MAKING SENS
MILITANT IS

'In Brief' Series: Books for Busy People

by Anne Davison

Copyright2015 Anne Davison

Books for Busy People

Other books in the 'In Brief' Series by Anne Davison

Abraham's Children: Christian Jew Muslim, Commonality and Conflict

From the Medes to the Mullahs: a History of Iran

Paul of Tarsus: a First Century Radical

The Holy Roman Empire: Power Politics Papacy

TABLE OF CONTENTS

MAPS AND CHARTS

PROLOGUE

The impetus for writing this book was sparked by an event that occurred on 19 August, 2014. On that day, television images showing American journalist James Foley being beheaded by a member of ISIS, also known as ISIL (Islamic State of Iraq and the Levant) or IS (Islamic State) were flashed around the world. To add to the horror expressed by the 'West', and especially Britain, was the fact that the perpetrator was reported as being a British jihadist from the London area.

Together with thousands of others I asked myself what had led this young man to leave his home, family and friends and travel to Syria in order to join a brutal terrorist organisation? Even worse, this is an organisation that unashamedly kills or enslaves not only non-Muslims, but also those who reject their particular version of Islam. There is probably no single or simple answer to this question but one thing that seems to be common to all jihadists of whatever group they belong, is a conviction that they are obeying the Will of God, or Allah.

Many books have been written about the various jihadist groups that have risen in recent decades. Most of these are the work of journalists or diplomats with first-hand experience of countries such as Afghanistan, Pakistan and other Middle Eastern countries. These books have tended to focus on the political background to militant Islam.

Politics certainly plays a part; none of these jihadist groups have emerged out of a political vacuum. On the contrary, radical groups have usually arisen in direct response to regional or international events.

Groups such as ISIS are self-professing Muslims claiming to follow a pure form of Islam in accordance to the Will of Allah. However, mainstream Muslims from around the world have condemned the actions of ISIS and they have also denounced their form of extremism as being un-Islamic.

The extreme version of Islam claimed by those who join ISIS is far removed from my understanding of Islam, both resulting from my own study of the Faith and from my experience of living with Muslims as neighbours, friends and colleagues.

I decided to explore for myself the roots of this extremism that has resulted in what many Muslims believe to be a dangerous distortion of the true Faith. I also wanted to try and make sense of the various jihadist groups around the world today. For example, what are the differences between the Taliban, the Muslim Brotherhood, Al Qaeda, ISIS and others?

This book is an attempt to address these questions. Unlike other books that focus on either the politics or the theology, this book will explore the religious dimension in the context of political events. Indeed, this approach is essential since in Islam religion and politics have been inseparable since the time of the Prophet in the 6th century.

I have entitled this book *Making Sense of Militant Islam*. This title begs the question: what is militant Islam as opposed to radical Islam, extremist Islam or political Islam? Today these terms are often interchangeable and indeed there are elements of overlap. One of the challenges of this book is an attempt to unravel these various 'Islamisms'.

Those readers who are interested in the theological and ideological thinking of militant Islamists will find chapters one to three helpful; readers wanting to know more about the recent growth in militant Islam will find chapters four onwards of particular interest.

As with other books in the series, this book is aimed at the general reader who wants to understand a particular historical topic but does not have the time or inclination to read a heavy academic tome. With this mind, footnotes have been omitted. However, the reader will find a small selection of the main works that have been consulted at the end. Also included is a short glossary of Islamic terms.

Finally, I would like to thank those friends and colleagues who gave of their time to read through various chapters, proof read the script, and offered helpful comments.

INTRODUCTION

In all religious traditions there is diversity in terms of belief and practice. Islam is no exception and very early in its history divisions that were fuelled by both political events and questions of faith became evident among the nascent *Ummah* (Community of the Faithful).

The early Church faced similar difficulties in 325 CE, when the Roman Emperor Constantine called a church Council in Nicaea, modern Turkey. Some 312 bishops from across Christendom attended the council, known as the First Ecumenical Council. The task facing the bishops was to resolve disagreements over Christian doctrine in the hope that this would also lead to political stability across the Empire.

Both Christianity and Islam faced conflicts over authority. For Christians the issue related to doctrinal authority regarding the nature of Christ. For Muslims it was a question of leadership and who had the authority to lead the *Ummah* following the death of Muhammad in 632 CE.

In both situations the outcome eventually led to disagreements and schisms. The party of consensus, being the majority, became the mainstream 'orthodox' group while those who rejected the majority view became minority 'heretical' sects. This is a pattern that can be seen within all Faiths and is repeated throughout history.

Another pattern that repeats itself is the way that religious thought and practice is influenced by historical events. In other words, outside events, secular as well as political can impinge upon a religious community so forcing that tradition to rethink or reform its theology.

This can be particularly difficult for adherents of the three monotheistic Faiths of Judaism, Christianity and Islam, all of which have a high view of the Hebrew Scriptures, the Bible and the Qur'an respectively.

For each of these Faiths their Holy Scripture is believed to be the revealed Word of God and therefore holds a place of high authority. Many people of faith will therefore look to their Holy Scripture as a guide for their lives or even as justification for a particular action.

However, all three Faiths face a similar problem. Their religious texts were formulated hundreds, if not thousands of years ago and therefore do not necessarily speak to the world of the 21st century.

Many of the divisions across all three Faiths have arisen over the issue of how to interpret ancient Scripture for today's world. Those of a liberal persuasion will often be flexible in their interpretation in order to make it 'fit' into a current situation or modern worldview.

Probably the majority of people within all three Faiths will take a middle road and therefore compromise between the opposing liberal and conservative views. Some people will change their position depending on the context. For example, they may take a liberal stance on the question of abortion but an extremely conservative view regarding homosexuality.

Generally speaking, those of a conservative persuasion will adopt a more literalist approach towards a religious text, resulting in an uncomfortable situation whereby the text and the majority worldview are irreconcilable. This is where we will find adherents of militant Islam. Common across all extremist Islamic groups is a particular interpretation of the Qur'an that is incompatible with modern society but is considered as having ultimate authority.

In the first part of this book we will look at the Qur'an and the *hadith* (tradition; deeds and sayings of the Prophet) and the development of the various schools of jurisprudence in terms of authority.

The succession crisis following the death of Muhammad resulted in a theological debate that was centred on the nature of authority in terms of who should lead the *Ummah.* This issue also has particular relevance today in that ISIS claims to have established a Caliphate, the legitimacy of which would be challenged by the majority of Muslims around the world.

Chapter Three explores how the doctrine of militant *jihad* was developed by key Muslim thinkers in response to the Mongol invasions of the 13th century. Chapter Four outlines the development of Arab Nationalism following the collapse of the Ottoman Empire and the Arab reaction to European imperialism.

The final chapters examine the rise of militant Islamism in the 20th century including the founding of the Muslim Brotherhood, the *Taliban, Al-Qaeda* and ISIS. For the sake of consistency the term ISIS will be used in preference to ISIL or IS.

CHAPTER ONE
By What Authority?
The Qur'an and *Hadith*

Introduction

For Muslims the Qur'an, Islam's Holy Scripture, holds ultimate authority. Believed to be the Word of God that was revealed to the Prophet Muhammad in the 7th Century, the text offers guidance for Muslims of all traditions and for every aspect of life.

Next to the Qur'an is the *hadith*, a collection of the sayings and deeds of the Prophet. The early scholars based the *Shari'a* (religious law) on a combination of the Qur'an and *hadith*.

As Islam spread beyond the Arabian Peninsula into new cultural and political situations, different *madhhabs* (schools of law) emerged with different views on the authority of the *hadiths*.

The various jihadist groups that represent militant Islam today tend to follow one particular narrow strand of Islamic thought that can be traced back to *Ahmad Ibn Hanbal* who founded the *Hanbali madhhab* at the beginning of the 9th century.

The Qur'an.

When Muhammad was about 40 years old, in 610 CE, he had a religious experience that is traditionally accepted as a revelation from God. While seeking solitude in a cave on Mount *Hira,* close to Mecca, it is said that the Angel Gabriel visited him and commanded him, in the name of God, to recite:

Read! In the name of your Lord who created.

He created man from a clinging form.

Read! Your Lord Is the Most Bountiful One

who taught by pen,

who taught man what he did not know.

These five verses form the first part of *sura* (chapter) 96 and are believed by Muslims to be the first verses of the Qur'an (meaning 'recite' or 'read') that were revealed to Muhammad.

The revelations continued intermittently for some 23 years until the Prophet's death in 632 CE, by which time 114 *suras* had been revealed. Some of these *suras* were transmitted while Muhammad was in Mecca and others while he was in Medina towards the end of his life. It is interesting to note that the later *suras* appear more militant in tone than the earlier text when the Prophet and his followers were in a minority situation. Today's militant Islamists tend to refer to these later verses when looking for justification for their own actions.

The content of the Qur'an includes aspects of Islamic Faith such as the existence of God, stories about the Hebrew Prophets as well as Jesus and His mother Mary. Other topics include charitable giving, prayer, a stress on ethical and moral issues and the importance of discerning right from wrong.

It is generally accepted that Muhammad was illiterate and that as the *suras* were revealed his Companions acted as scribes as he dictated to them what he had heard. After the Prophet's death his successor, the first Caliph (Successor), *Abu Bakr,* began to collect the various texts together.

By the time of *Uthman,* the third Caliph, who ruled from 644 CE to 656 CE, Islam had spread beyond the Arabian Peninsula into non-Arab lands. As a result, the correct pronunciation of the Qur'an was becoming corrupted, a situation that could lead to a subtle change in the meaning of the text. *Uthman*, who was an older, scholarly man, therefore ordered the compilation of a standard text to be used by all Muslims regardless of location or ethnic origin.

By about 650 CE *Uthman's* Qur'an had become the 'standard' text from which all subsequent versions were copied. Although a few alternative texts have existed at different times, *Uthman's* Codex has remained the generally accepted text for Muslims down the centuries and across the world.

While there may be different views on interpretation, the majority of Muslims believe that the Qur'an represents the word of God as revealed to the Prophet Muhammad. Crucially the Revelation was received in Arabic and was subsequently transmitted and written down by the Companions in Arabic.

Consequently Muslims worldwide, regardless of sect, ethnic background or native language, will read, study and recite the Qur'an in Arabic, since any attempt to translate the Holy Scripture into another language could result in an inauthentic text. This can result in a situation, particularly in the West among non-Arabic speaking Muslims, whereby the student or worshipper may not fully understand the meaning of the text, nor more crucially not hear the words of God as He spoke to Muhammad.

The Qur'an as created

While there appears to be a universal understanding within Islam that the Qur'an is the revealed Word of God, there have been differences of opinion regarding the nature of the Qur'an. For example, as early as the 8th century theologians debated whether or not the Qur'an was created or was co-eternal with God.

The former group, who claimed that the Qur'an was created, were known as the *Mu'tazilis* (those who kept themselves apart). They believed that through a process of reason the truths of the Qur'an could be discerned. The *Mu'tazilis* were strong for a time under the Abbasid Caliphate of *Ma'mum* (813-833 CE), which was a period when the Muslim community became influenced by the rational and philosophical thought of the newly conquered Byzantines. The *Mu'tazilis* were later to influence the Shi'a and Sufi traditions.

The Qur'an as co-eternal

The majority opinion of the early Islamic community was that undue emphasis on reason could be dangerous and lead to disputes. This group believed that the Qur'an was the eternal, uncreated Word of God and that the Qur'an, together with the tradition of the Prophet and his Companions, known as the *sunna*, was sufficient guidance for the community.

The theologian who is best known for rejecting the rationalism of the *Mu'tazilis* is *Ahmad ibn Hanbal* (780-855 CE). His preaching and teaching, which was at that time in opposition to that of Caliph *al Ma'mun*, led to his imprisonment and he was only released when a later Caliph, *al Mu'tasim*, who was also unsympathetic to the *Mu'tazilis*, came to the throne.

The *Hadith*

Soon after the death of the Prophet his followers began collecting various sayings and actions that were attributable to him. So began another body of literature that became known as *hadith*, meaning the tradition of the Prophet according to his sayings and actions. Since Muhammad was to become the role model for all Muslims it was necessary to have as much information as possible about his life so that this information could provide a guide for the community.

The *hadith* is divided into two parts, one being the narrative or account of the words and deeds of the Prophet, the other providing a chain of reliable witnesses to the particular saying or action. These witnesses were traced chronologically back to the life of Muhammad.

Arab society in the 6th century was oral and all the *hadiths* were originally orally transmitted. As a result, both content and witness were open to error, which in turn led to the need for *hadith*-criticism. The scholars who undertook this task paid particular attention to the trust-worthiness or otherwise of the witnesses. The *hadiths* were then categorised as being: a) sound/authentic, b) weak or c) fabricated.

One of the most reliable collections of *hadith* that is widely recognised across the Muslim world is the work of *al-Bukhari* who was born in Bukhara, Khorasan in 810 CE and died in Samarkand, Uzbekistan in 870 CE.

The *Sunni* and the *Shi'a* have different corpus of *hadith* that reflects the schism between the two sects that occurred in the 7th century. This schism is described in an earlier book in this series (*Abraham's Children: Jew Christian Muslim Commonality and Conflict*) and will be covered in the following chapter.

Briefly, the *Sunni* accept all the *hadiths* of the first four Caliphs and also that of Muhammad's wife *Aisha*. However, since the *Shi'a* reject the authority of the first three Caliphs they naturally reject the *hadiths* of those witnesses. Furthermore, the *Shi'a* have an extremely low regard for *Aisha* and would consider her *hadiths* to be weak, or even more likely, fabricated.

The *Madhhabs*

The Qur'an and *hadith* were rooted in Arab culture and from the beginning there was no separation between secular law and religious law. Therefore, when Islam spread beyond the Arabian Peninsula it was necessary to integrate the local customs and traditions of the newly conquered territories into Islamic law. This was to be the task of the *Qadi* (religious judge) and the *ulema* (religious scholars and clerics). The religious scholars based their judgments on the Qur'an, the *hadith* and the tradition or consensus of the early Islamic community.

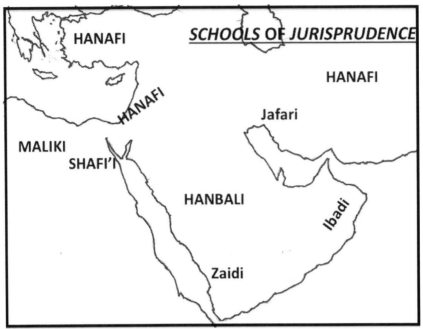

By the middle of the 9th century four major schools of Islamic jurisprudence, or law, known as *madhhabs*, had emerged within the *Sunni* tradition across the Muslim world. These were known as the *Hanafi, the Maliki*, the *Shafi'i,* and the *Hanbali,* each school taking its name from its founder. The *Shi'a* had their own *madhhabs*, known as the *Jafari and Zaidi.* The *Ibadi* is a separate *madhhab* that has its roots and practice in Oman.

```
┌─────────────────────────────────────────────────────────┐
│                                                           │
│   ISLAMIC SCHOOLS OF JURISPRUDENCE (Law)                  │
│              (Madhhabs)                                   │
│                                                           │
│       Sunni                        Shi'a                  │
│                                                           │
│      HANAFI                        ISMAILI                │
│      HANBALI                       JAFARI                 │
│      MALIKI                        ZAIDI                  │
│      SHAFI'I                                              │
│                      IBADI                                │
│                     (Oman)                                │
│                                                           │
└─────────────────────────────────────────────────────────┘
```

Imam Abu Hanifa, (699-767 CE), the first of the founders, was born in Kufa, modern Iraq and was probably of Persian origin. Being born only 66 years after the death of Muhammad he had been able to meet some of the Companions of the Prophet. It is believed that he received *hadith* directly from them, which gives him a very high status in terms of authority. The *Hanafi* School is named after him and is followed by the majority of Muslims in the world.

Imam Malik, (711-795 CE) lived his entire life in Medina and is highly revered on account of his 'chain of witnesses'. For example, Muhammad narrated to *Umar,* who was the second Caliph, who then narrated to *Nafi* who in turn narrated to *Malik.* This places the scholar just two witnesses removed from the Prophet. The majority of Muslims in North Africa follow the *Maliki* School.

Imam Shafi, (767-820 CE) was born in Gaza and spent some time studying in Medina under *Imam Malik.* After a period in Baghdad he finally settled in Egypt where he established his school of jurisprudence. He was known to promote the use of human reasoning along with the 'revealed' word of the Qur'an and *hadith*. Followers of the *Shafi'i Madhhab* can today be found in Indonesia, Malaysia, Sri Lanka and South India.

Imam Ahmad Ibn Hanba,l (780-855 CE) was the last of the four great scholars and he was born in Baghdad at a crucial time in the history of Islam. Just thirty years before his birth the *Abbasids,* who descended from the Prophet's youngest uncle, *Abbas ibn Abd al-Muttalib* (566 - 653 CE), overthrew the *Umayyad* dynasty and moved the capital of the Caliphate from Damascus to Baghdad from where they ruled from 750 to 1517 CE.

The change of dynasty from the *Umayyads* to the *Abbasids* was not only a change in power but it also marked a change in cultural influence, away from its Arabian heritage into a Byzantine/Greek/Persian world. This led to a period known as Islam's Golden Age witnessing a synthesis of Greek and Arab culture that resulted in great scientific, philosophical and cultural flowering.

In this new climate of philosophical and religious tolerance, that encouraged the use of logic and reason, radical new theologies emerged. Of particular importance were the *Mu'tazilis,* referred to above, who believed in the created nature of the Qur'an. In other words, they claimed that while Muhammad heard the Word of God, those words were then transcribed by human act. Consequently while the Word is divine, the Qur'an, as the written Word, is created.

This was totally contradictory to the teaching of *Ibn Hanbal* who believed that the Qur'an was uncreated and co-eternal with God. However, *Ibn Hanbal's* beliefs were not in line with the current thinking of the Abbasids and resulted in him being summoned before the Caliph *al Ma'mun* who demanded that he recant his views. When the scholar refused he was imprisoned, as mentioned above.

Ibn Hanbal is revered for his commitment to the early *Sunni* traditions of the first generations of Muslims. Followers of the

Hanbali School can be found today in Saudi Arabia, Qatar, the Emirates, with minority groups in Syria and Iraq.

Of interest to us is that an element of today's militant Islamists, for example the *Wahabbis* and *Salafis*, both of whom will be discussed later, can be traced back to the *Hanbali* doctrines of the 8th century.

The Importance of the *Madhhabs*

The four main *Sunni madhhabs* were founded in the early period of Islamic history in response to the needs of the *qadis* (judges) and *ulema* (clerics) whose responsibility it was to formulate the *Sharia* for the growing number of believers across the Empire. While the early schools shared much in common, any differences usually reflected the social and cultural setting of the particular community.

Each of the founders of the four schools took as their source material the text of the Qur'an and the *hadith* that was composed of hundreds and thousands of different sayings. The early scholars travelled widely collecting *hadith,* all the while constantly checking the authenticity and reliability of the witnesses.

The next task was to check each *hadith* against both the Qur'an and other *hadiths.* The checks concerned such things as names, dates and events. Where inconsistencies appeared, whether within the Qur'anic text or across different *hadiths,* further study was required. A particular task was to assess whether or not an early ruling had been superseded by a later text, a situation that frequently occurred.

From the very beginning Islam has always placed great emphasis upon learning with the expectation that all Muslims, female as well as male, should study the Qur'an and *hadith.* However, it has equally been acknowledged that the task of making judgments in accordance with Islamic law can only be the preserve of those scholars who are qualified for the task, in other words the *qadi* and the *ulema.*

These scholars did not work in isolation but learned from other scholars within the same school or even those from a different school. For example, we saw above that *Imam Shafi* studied for a while under *Imam Malik*. In this way particular theological traditions developed and all later scholars and *Imams* would generally identify with one particular school of jurisprudence or *madhhab.*

The *madhhabs* therefore provide a system of sound scholarship, which is ongoing, against which Islamic Faith and practice can be measured. Today, however, there are signs that some Muslims regard the *madhhabs* as irrelevant, claiming that the Qur'an and *hadith* are sufficient. In other words they disregard the wealth of Islamic scholarship that has sustained the Faith for centuries. The result is that such Muslims take a literal view of the Qur'an together with unreliable *hadith.*

This would be the position of most adherents of militant Islam today. Their understanding of the Faith is limited and has led to an extremism that the majority of mainstream Muslims reject as being un-Islamic.

As a result they will take their chosen text as authoritative while there may well be later scholarship that is accepted by mainstream Islam offering quite a different meaning to the text.

An example here would be the desecration of graves that some groups have carried out believing that this is what Muhammad commanded during his lifetime. According to most scholars, this only applied at a time when the Arabian Peninsula was still populated by pagan, idolatrous tribes. It does not apply to the graves of the Companions or Muslim saints.

Sheik Nur Ha Mim Keller highlighted the seriousness of the situation whilst on a lecture tour of the United States, Canada and England during 1994 and 1995 when he said:

'It cannot be hidden from any of you how urgent this issue is, or that many of the disagreements we see and hear in our mosques these days are due to lack of knowledge of fiqh or "Islamic jurisprudence" and its relation to Islam as a whole. Now, perhaps

more than ever before, it is time for us to get back to basics and ask ourselves how we understand and carry out the commands of Allah.

Without a guiding hand, the untrained reader will misunderstand many of the hadiths he reads... Such a person is particularly easy prey for modern sectarian movements of our times appearing in a neo-orthodox guise, well financed and published, quoting Quran and hadiths to the uninformed to make a case for the basic contention of all deviant sects since the beginning of Islam.'

Conclusion

This chapter has looked at the Qur'an, the *hadith* and the schools of jurisprudence, or *madhhabs* in terms of authority. The Qur'an, as the revealed Word of God, takes primacy. The *hadith*, being the sayings and actions of Muhammad, is also considered an authoritative body of literature to be studied alongside the Qur'an. The early Islamic scholars categorised the *hadith* according to reliability.

As Islam spread beyond the Arabian Peninsula the scholars were faced with the task of integrating local cultural practices into Islamic law (*sharia*). This resulted in the founding of four distinct schools of jurisprudence. An extremely important task of the scholars was to discern how a particular text might have been superseded by a later text or *hadith*.

While Muslims are encouraged to study the Qur'an and *hadith* individually, the importance of qualified teachers, preachers or *imams* has always been stressed. These *imams* would normally follow the tradition of a particular school of jurisprudence. It follows therefore that the Qur'an may be interpreted differently according to first, the use of particular *hadith* and second, according to the particular *madhhab*. This is why we see a great cultural and religious diversity across the Muslim world.

The concern today is that the various radical groups disregard the *madhhabs* and have a very limited understanding of the Qur'an and *hadith*. Consequently, they will select certain texts from the Qur'an as authority for *jihad*, murder and other terrorist activities.

CHAPTER TWO

By Whose Authority?

The Caliph and Caliphate

Introduction

The previous chapter looked at the authoritative nature of the Qur'an, the *hadith* and the importance of the schools of jurisprudence.

This chapter will explore the nature of authority in terms of leadership. For example, who has the right to rule? How is a ruler chosen? Can he - and in Islamic history it has usually been 'he' - be deposed? What is the role of the caliph and how is power delegated?

There have been three major caliphates, which are Islamic states governed by *Sharia* Law under the leadership of a religious and political leader known as a caliph. All three caliphates stretched across several continents and were the central focus of authority for the majority of Muslims at the time.

They were the *Umayyads* (661-750 CE), the *Abbasids* (750-1258 CE) and the Ottomans (1299-1923 CE). There were also several minor Caliphate*s*, for example the *Fatimids* of Egypt (909 - 1171 CE) and the Caliphate of Cordoba in Spain (929–1031 CE). In both Egypt and Spain jurisdiction was restricted to the local region. Some parts of the world, such as Indonesia, have never been part of central caliphate or *Ummah.*

When Kemal Ataturk, leader of the newly founded Turkish state, dissolved the Ottoman Caliphate on 3 March 1924, a focal point for Islamic authority was lost. There are many Muslims across the world today who would like to see the revival of the caliphate. One such group is the self-proclaimed 'Caliphate' of IS, otherwise known as the Islamic State. IS sees itself as the revived Caliphate, but on what authority?

The Succession Crisis

The word Caliph comes from the Arabic word *khalifa,* meaning 'successor'. When the Prophet Muhammad died of natural causes on 8 June 632 CE, aged about 62 years, he had no son to succeed him and he had not publicly named a successor. This left the nascent Islamic community in a state of chaos and confusion as to who should succeed as leader of the *Ummah.*

It was this issue that would eventually lead to the split into the two main sects of Islam, the *Sunni* (those who followed the *Sunnah*, or 'way of the Prophet') and the *Shi'a* (those who followed Ali, or the 'Party of Ali').

The closest male relative to Muhammad was Ali, who was his cousin, being the son of his uncle Abu Talib. When Abu Talib found himself in financial difficulty Muhammad took the young Ali into his household as his adopted son and from that moment on the two were extremely close. The relationship was further strengthened when Ali later married Muhammad's daughter Fatima.

Although not a blood relative, it would have been normal in Arab society at the time for Ali to succeed Muhammad on the grounds that he was the closest male relative. But there were those in the community who were opposed to the idea. In a society that respected age, some felt that at 25 years, Ali was simply too young.

Others objected on the grounds that if Ali was chosen this would be a dynastic succession, which was unacceptable in a society that was opposed to any kind of dynastic or monarchical rule since the Muslims believed that only God could rule as 'King'. This was to change in later centuries of Islamic history when many Caliphs ruled with all the trappings of a royal court.

Indeed, it is this very issue that many of today's radical groups challenge. They would say that those who claim to rule as 'King', for example the King of Saudi Arabia, the King of Jordan or the 'Shah' in pre-revolutionary Iran, are acting against the basic tenets of Islam as set down by Muhammad. They are, therefore, illegitimate as rulers and deserve to be deposed.

An added complication to the succession crisis of the 7th century was the fact that Muhammad had not been explicit as to who should succeed him on his death. The *Shi'a*, however, have always claimed that on several occasions the Prophet, through his words and actions, had indicated that he wished Ali to be his successor.

Three different groups emerged, each claiming the rights of succession.

The first group were the 'Emigrants', Muhammad's first followers, the majority of whom had travelled with him from Mecca to Medina in 622 CE. This event is known as the *Hijra*, meaning the 'flight' or 'migration' and the date marks the beginning of the Islamic calendar. Those who accompanied the Prophet to Medina became known as the Companions.

Muhammad and his Companions, who were the first Muslims, left Mecca for Medina because their lives were in danger. They had been suffered persecution from the wealthy and powerful *Quraish* tribe who controlled both Mecca and the lucrative pilgrimage trade at the *Kaaba*. Muhammad's preaching had challenged the pagan lifestyle of the *Quraish*, had led to growing numbers joining the Muslims and generally created instability resulting in a loss of trade for the *Quraish*.

The concept of the *Hijra* in terms of migrating to a place where it is possible to live freely as Muslims is still present today. In recent weeks (August 2014) several young Muslims, both male and female, have been interviewed on British television stating that they were travelling to Syria to join the Islamic State because they wanted the freedom to live their lives fully under *Sharia* Law.

The second group were the inhabitants of Medina known as the *Ansar* or 'helpers', so named because of the help and hospitality they offered Muhammad with his Companions when they first arrived in Medina.

It was during the ten years spent in Medina that Muhammad laid down the principles of the Islamic Faith based upon the on-going revelations that he received from God through the Angel Gabriel. This was a foundational period for Islam. It is a period that many Muslims, particularly modern Islamists, see as a time when the 'pure' Faith was practiced before corruption began to set in.

The third group were leading Meccan families of the *Quraish* tribe, the majority of whom were later converts to Islam.

The First Four Caliphs (*the Rashidun*)

THE FIRST FOUR CALIPHS
The Rashidun (Rightly Guided Ones)
Quoraish Tribe

Abu Bakr (Abdullah ibn Abi Quhafa)	632-634
Umar (Umar ibn Al-Khattab)	634-644
Uthman (Uthman ibn 'Affan)	644-656
Ali (Ali ibn Abu Talib)	656-661

Abu Bakr, the First *Caliph*

Immediately after the Prophet's death, while Ali and the immediate family were preparing for the burial, the inhabitants of Medina, the *Ansar* or 'Helpers', called a *Shura* (Council of Elders) to discuss the question of succession. Because the *Shura* was arranged so quickly the Emigrants (those who had made the *Hijra* from Mecca) arrived late. Significantly, Ali was not present.

According to Albert Hourani, in his book *A History of the Arab Peoples*, Abu Bakr, one of the closest Companions and father-in-law of Muhammad, proclaimed:

O men, if you worship Muhammad, Muhammad is dead; if you worship God, God is alive.

Abu Bakr was making the point that Muhammad should not be worshipped since he was purely human. However, there was still a need to find a leader to act as an arbiter and decision maker. In no way, however, would the new leader be a Prophet. Central to Islamic thought is that Muhammad was the final Prophet, one of a long line of Prophets beginning with Abraham. Muhammad was the Seal of the Prophets.

The *shura* chose Abu Bakr to be Successor (*Khalifa*/Caliph) to the Messenger of God. He was a member of the first group of contenders, one of the Emigrants, a close Companion and father of Muhammad's second wife Aisha.

The rule of Abu Bakr, which lasted just two years from 632 to 634 CE, ushered in a period known as the *Rashidun*, meaning the 'Rightly Guided Ones'. It was a period of relatively just government enabling Islam to spread beyond the Arabian Peninsula into the Levant, North Africa and Mesopotamia.

Within months of the death of the Prophet, Abu Bakr was faced with rebellion from some of the tribes who had previously sworn allegiance to both Muhammad and Islam. The tribes assumed that their loyalty ended with the death of Muhammad and they could therefore stop paying tribute and taxes.

This was the first test of authority faced by the Caliphate. Abu Bakr settled the issue by sending an army to put down the various revolts, reassert Islamic authority and re-impose taxes and tribute on the rebellious tribes. This period of instability became known as the *Ridda*, or Apostasy Wars.

Umar ibn Al-Khattab, the Second Caliph

Abu Bakr died of natural causes in August 634 CE. In order to avoid a repeat of the earlier problems over succession, he nominated Umar ibn Al-Khattab as the next Caliph. Under Umar, Islam spread northeast into the Sassanid Empire and within two years the whole of Persia was conquered. At the same time almost two thirds of the Christian Byzantine Empire came under Islamic rule including the Levant and Syria.

Umar achieved much during his ten-year rule, the greatest being the expansion of the Islamic Empire. But in the process of conquering Persia he created many enemies. A group of aggrieved Persians plotted to kill him while he was leading prayers at the main mosque in Medina. One of them, a slave, stabbed him six times in the stomach and he died of his wounds three days later.

Umar chose not to name a successor but as he lay on his deathbed he ordered that the decision should be left in the hands of a *Shura*. He appointed a selection committee of six, with instructions that the group should choose one of the six, which included Ali, as the next Caliph. He also instructed that the group should meet in closed session, be guarded and that they should make their decision within three days.

Among the six candidates Ali had little support and he was once more over-looked. Instead, the elderly aristocrat Uthman was chosen, most likely as an interim choice. The assumption was that he would not live long, but long enough to give time for the other candidates to muster support for their preferred candidacy.

Uthman ibn Affan, the Third Caliph

Uthman reigned for an unexpected period of 12 years during which time the Islamic Empire spread in the West to Morocco and in the East to Pakistan and Azerbaijan. He also sent diplomatic missions to China and Sri Lanka.

However, Uthman made the mistake of appointing close members of his family and others of the Umayyad clan of Mecca into senior positions across the Empire, often as governors of garrison towns such as Basra and Kufa in modern Iraq and Fustat (now Cairo) in Egypt. He built magnificent palaces and adopted the court life of the Byzantines. In the eyes of many, Uthman had moved away from the simple life as taught and exemplified by Muhammad. In other words he had become a corrupt ruler and calls for his abdication grew among the *Ummah*.

Uthman ignored such demands and eventually a group from Medina and other garrison towns plotted his assassination. On 20 June 656 CE rebels broke into Uthman's house and he was bludgeoned to death. Ali and his sons, Hasan and Husayn, had been among those trying to protect the Caliph's house from the attackers. Immediately Uthman was declared dead the crowd called for Ali to be elected the new Caliph.

Ali ibn Abi Talib, the Fourth Caliph

When he succeeded to the Caliphate, Ali inherited all the problems inherent within the *Ummah* that had contributed to Uthman's assassination. However he was dedicated to the Prophet's teaching on equality and justice and his aim now was to eradicate the bad practices put in place by Uthman, particularly that of nepotism.

But perhaps the greatest difficulty he faced was how to deal with the growing calls for revenge against the murderers of Uthman. Uthman was a member of the *Umayyad* clan of the powerful *Quraish* tribe and, as was usual practice at the time, the *Umayyads* were now calling for immediate revenge. However, Ali was reluctant to punish the assassins because Uthman was in many ways a corrupt leader who had refused all calls to step down. In other words his 'removal', even by assassination, might have been justified.

Ali was in a difficult situation. His refusal to succumb to calls for revenge led to on-going conflict between the *Umayyads* and the *Ahl al-Bayt* (his own House of the Prophet): conflict that was later to contribute to the *Sunni-Shia* schism. The situation confronting Ali called into question the role of the Caliph and how to deal with despotic rulers. It was a theme that was to be echoed throughout Islamic history.

Ali attempted to heal the rift with the *Umayyads* through dialogue. However, one group, known as the *Kharijites* (meaning 'those who went out') saw this as an abrogation of his duty as

Caliph believing that Ali should hold firm against the rebels. Consequently they plotted his assassination and he was attacked while praying in the mosque in Kufa, modern Iraq. He died of his wounds a few days later on 31 January 661 CE.

Some Muslims take the view that the Caliphate ended with the death of Ali. Their reasoning is that he was the last of the Caliphs to hold universal authority over the Muslim world. Furthermore, while the majority *Sunni* Muslims recognise all four of the *Rashidun* Caliphs, the *Shi'a* only acknowledge the legitimacy of Ali's Caliphate.

The Authority of the Caliph

From the time of the Prophet's death in 632 CE the *Ummah* struggled over the question of succession. How much and what authority should the Caliph have? How should he be chosen? What qualities were expected of any prospective candidate?

While the Caliph was in no way a prophet, he was the political leader of the Islamic community who would be expected to rule in accordance with the Qur'an and the *Sharia*. Later Caliphs assumed authority for secular and religious life beyond the strictures of the Qur'an.

In the early period, the Islamic community was quite clear that there could only ever be one Caliph ruling at any one time. According to a *Hadith* of Abu Bakr, Muhammad's successor and closest friend:

'It is forbidden for Muslims to have two Amirs for this would cause differences in their affairs and concepts, their unity would be divided and disputes would break out amongst them.'

Umar bin Al-Khattab, another disciple, is reported as saying *'There is no way for two (leaders) together at any one time'.*

These statements referred to the early Caliphate when Muslim territory was limited to the Arabian Peninsula and the Levant. Furthermore, it is not surprising that Abu Bakr and Umar expressed such a view since they were both Caliphs and protective of their power.

In the 12th century, by which time Islam had spread well beyond the Arabian Peninsula into North Africa and Mesopotamia, Imam Al-Nawawi of the *Shafi'i madhhab* said *'It is forbidden to give an oath to two caliphs or more, even in different parts of the world and even if they are far apart'.* This statement clearly reflects the fact that alternative Caliphates were being declared.

Succession theory and practice

The first four Caliphs were chosen through a process of consensus. With the death of Ali the *Ummah* divided into two opposing views regarding succession. One group, the *Shi'a* believed that the succession should be passed on through the line of the House of the Prophet via Ali, to his son Hasan. The second, and largest group, the *Sunni* believed that the Caliph should be chosen by consensus. The *Kharijites* rejected both views claiming that the Caliphate should go to the person best qualified, regardless of pedigree.

Around the beginning of the 12th century the respected Muslim scholar and philosopher, *Al Ghazali* (1058-1111), wrote the *Nasihat al-Muluk* (Advice for Kings). His treatise was aimed at the Caliph and contained ethical guidelines for good governance, for example:

'The ruler should understand the importance and danger of the authority entrusted to him.'

'The ruler should always be thirsting to meet devout religious scholars and ask them for advice.'

'The ruler should make the utmost effort to behave gently and avoid governing harshly.'

Another issue that has repeatedly presented itself throughout the history of Islam is the potential conflict between the Caliph and *Ulema.* In theory it has been the duty of the Caliph to rule the people, while the *Ulema* has authority over all religious issues including the interpretation of Islamic Law. However, the boundary between the two may not always be clear.

Conclusion

In this chapter we have looked at the emergence of the Caliphate following the death of Muhammad. From the beginning, it was clear that while the Caliph was the arbiter and leader of the community as successor to the Prophet, he was neither a prophet nor a messenger of God.

The greatest challenge facing the *Ummah* was less to do with the Caliph's role but more about how he should be chosen. In slightly different ways all four of the first Caliphs were chosen by consensus and are known as the 'Rightly Guided Ones' (*Rashidun*). A related issue, as was the case with *Uthman*, was how to deal with a despotic or unjust ruler.

The first four Caliphs were at the time the sole rulers of the *Ummah*. Many Muslims of the *Sunni* tradition believe that when the fourth Caliph, Ali, died this marked the end of the Caliphate. They claim that the legitimacy of a Caliph is only valid if he rules over the universal, or worldwide community of believers.

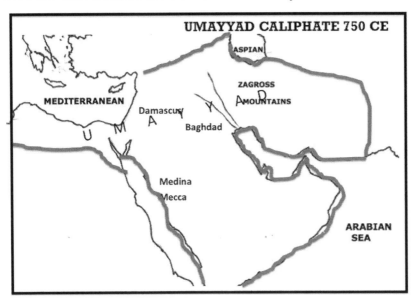

Although there have been several Caliphates since the 7th century, the most important being the *Fatimids* and the

Ottomans, none held universal jurisdiction over all Muslims worldwide.

The most recent self-proclaimed Caliphate of the so-called Islamic State (IS) aims to rule over an area comparable with that of the early *Umayyad* dynasty. But the so-called Caliph of IS, *Abu Bakr al-Baghdadi,* was not elected by the *Ummah* and therefore is not recognised as having any legitimacy by the majority of Muslims. If this is the case by what, or on whose, authority does IS claim to rule?

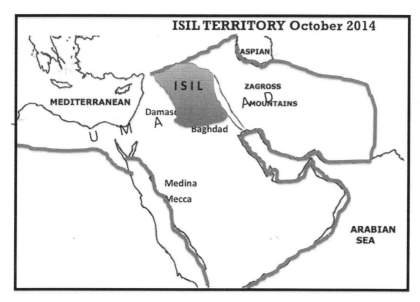

CHAPTER THREE

Challenge to Authority

Ibn Taymiyya and *Al Wahhab*

Introduction

In the first chapter we considered the authority of the Qur'an and the *hadith.* The second chapter examined the authority of the Caliph and Caliphate. In both chapters an attempt was made to identify points of departure between the authoritative mainstream 'orthodox' position of early Islam (*Sunna)* and that of some modern militant Islamist groups.

This chapter looks at the beginnings of theological dissent and diversity that was an inevitable outcome of an expanding empire. Some of those groups espousing new ways of thinking have always been viewed as a challenge to the authority of the *Ummah* and have consequently been considered heretical.

In the eyes of mainstream *Sunni* Islam heresy leads to factionalism and it is therefore a danger to the unity of the community of believers. Some conservative Muslims to this day, holding the same opinion, would regard both the *Shi'a* and the *Sufis* (those who practice a more mystical version of Islam) as heretical.

One way to deal with the problem of heresy was to reinforce the revealed word of Muhammad, the early *hadiths* and the tradition of the first generations of Muslims. In this respect *Ibn Hanbal* and the *Hanbali* School provided the best example of a way forward. *Ibn Hanbal* condemned all forms of 'innovation' (*bid'ah)* including philosophical speculation. His influence is still strong today among many radical groups but probably the first thinker of any importance to advocate the teaching of *Ibn Hanbal*, was *Ibn Taymiyya*.

Ibn Taymiyya (1263-1328) and *jihad*

Ibn Taymiyya was born in Haran, modern Turkey in 1263. Both his father and grandfather were Islamic scholars following the

Hanbali School of law. Early in his life he and his family moved from Haran to Damascus in Syria hoping to escape the Mongol invasions that were sweeping westwards across Central Asia. *Taymiyya* followed in the family tradition and became a renowned *Hanbali* scholar and frequently preached in the great *Umayyad* mosque of Damascus.

This was a time of political instability. Apart from the Mongol threat that lasted from 1241 for some 50 years, the region was also experiencing a change in dynastic rule. Around 1250 the *Mamluk* overthrew the *Ayyubid* Sultanate that had been founded in Cairo by *Saladin* in 1171 during the Crusader period.

The *Mamluks*, who were of Turkic origin, came from a region stretching from north of the Black Sea to the Caucasus. They were originally purchased as slaves and formed the backbone of the *Ayyubid* armies. By 1250 they had become so powerful that they were able to overthrow their *Ayyubid* masters. The Mamluks also defeated the European Crusaders in 1292 so marking the end of Crusader presence in the Holy Land after a period of some 200 years.

Ibn Taymiyya's thinking was therefore fine-tuned against the background of Mongol invasion, Christian Crusader occupation and *Mamluk* rule. In relation to the latter, although the *Mamluks* were Sunni Muslims, many were recent converts to Islam and had only a superficial understanding of the Faith. *Taymiyya* therefore took it upon himself to reassert the uncompromising foundational truths of Islam according to the *Hanbali* tradition. Apart from preaching and teaching he was also a prolific writer and many of his works are still available and have been translated into English.

Taymiyya's greatest challenge however, was how to deal with the Mongol threat and it was in response to this that he articulated a new understanding of *jihad.* Significantly, he placed a greater emphasis on the 'lesser *jihad*' (armed struggle) than the 'greater *jihad*' (the inner spiritual struggle within the self).

He declared that although the Mongols claimed to be Muslims, they did not live their lives according to the *Sharia* but instead continued to follow the written, or *Yasa*, law of their founder Genghis Khan. Consequently they were apostates against whom military *jihad* was not only permissible but indeed was the duty of every Muslim. He even went so far as to proclaim that waging *jihad* against the enemies of Islam was of equal importance to the five pillars of Islam that are incumbent on all Muslims, namely: Profession of Faith, Prayer, Almsgiving, Fasting and Pilgrimage.

Certainly *Ibn Taymiyya's* writings appear to extol the virtues of military *jihad*:

'It is allowed to fight people for [not observing] unambiguous and generally recognized obligations and prohibitions ... It is obligatory to take the initiative in fighting those people... But if they first attack the Muslims then fighting them is even more urgent.' (Rudolph Peters *Jihad in Classical and Modern Islam,* 1996)

Since the 9/11 terrorist bombing there have been attempts to link *Ibn Taymiyya's* theory of *jihad* with the ideology of *Al-Qaeda*. For example, *Al-Qaeda* has used *Taymiyya's* writings as justification for their own interpretation of *jihad* by equating the 13th century Mongols with the neo-Mongols of the 'West' and particularly the United States, a country that supports apostate regimes in the Middle East. In this latter respect Bin Laden particularly had in mind his own regime of Saudi Arabia that in his view was apostate because it permitted United States' forces to be based in the 'land of the two holy sites' (Mecca and Medina). Furthermore, these forces were to be used against Iraq, another Muslim country.

However, this theory is questioned in an essay by Camille Mulcaire, dated October 2013 that appeared on *E-International Relations,* a website set up for students and scholars of International Politics. Mulcaire claims that *Al-Qaeda's* interpretation of *Ibn Taymiyya* is a distortion of the scholar's words. For example, although *Taymiyya* supported military *jihad* in certain circumstances, he was explicit in that *'those who do not constitute a defensive or offensive power, like the women, the children, the monks, old people, the blind, and the permanently disabled should not be fought'.*

Mulcaire also points out that *Taymiyya* explicitly forbade violent rebellion against established Muslim leaders saying: '*if those in authority did not comply wholly with the orders of Allah, you should, anyway, obey them" since "sixty years domination of a despotic ruler are better than one single night passed without a ruler'.*

This ruling by *Taymiyya* is irreconcilable with the current view that despotic rulers such as Saddam Hussein, Colonel Gaddafi and President Assad should all be deposed. Furthermore, *Taymiyya's* words are strikingly prophetic in that Iraq and Libya, the leaders of which were deposed with the aid of the West, are now failed states. In Syria, opposition groups, again with the aid of the West, have attempted to depose President Assad. That country is now into its fourth year of civil war and large parts of Syria have been taken over by ISIS.

Ibn Taymiyya on other issues

Ibn Taymiyya had strong views regarding *the madhhabs* (schools of Islamic Jurisprudence) discussed in the previous chapter. While he respected the work of the scholars and the rightful place of jurisprudence, he condemned those who blindly followed the doctrines of a particular *madhhab* without reference to the Qur'an and *hadith.* He viewed this practice as similar to the way that Jews and Christians blindly follow their rabbis and priests and bishops of the ecclesiastical hierarchy, while making no attempt to learn from the basic texts for themselves. *Taymiyya's* elevation of the importance of the early texts over the teaching of the *madhhabs* is certainly a trend followed by modern Islamist groups.

Ibn Taymiyya recognised the special relationship that Muslims had with Jews and Christians as 'People of the Book' and as common descendants of Abraham, but he was opposed to borrowing anything from another religious tradition. Consequently, he opposed the celebration of the Prophet's birthday as being a practice that mirrored the Christian tradition of Christmas.

Although he had no problems with *Sufis* in principle, *Taymiyya* was extremely suspicious of some of their practices, for example the construction of tombs and veneration of *Sufi* saints. He believed that any form of veneration of prophets or saints amounted to *shirk* (idolatry). The desecration of tombs by those who consider them to be signs of idolatry has occurred throughout Islamic history.

At the present time such cases have become widespread at the hands of the so-called Islamic State who recently smashed the tomb of the Prophet Jonah in Mosul, Iraq. Those who carried out this destruction claim that their action was justified because the veneration of saints is un-Islamic. Their conviction no doubt has its roots in the teaching of *Ibn Taymiyya.*

Muhammad ibn Abd al-Wahhab (1703 – 1792)

A more recent scholar to have universal influence across the Islamic world is *Muhammad ibn Abd al-Wahhab* who was born in 1703 in the town of Uyayna in the Najd district of today's Saudi Arabia. In common with *Ibn Taymiyya* he was a scholar of the *Hanbali* tradition and much of his thinking mirrored that of *Ibn Taymiyya.*

It is common today to describe the growing number of radical and militant Islamist groups as *Wahhabis* meaning those who follow the teaching of *al-Wahhab*. However, since *Wahhabism* is used in a derogatory way, many Muslims, particularly in Saudi Arabia, refer to themselves as *Muwahhidin* (Unitarians) in recognition of their absolute commitment to monotheism. This is not to be confused with the Druze of the Levant who also refer to themselves as *Muwahhidin.*

Al-Wahhab was born into the *Banu Tamim,* which was a settled clan of the town. He began studying Islam with his father, who was also a *Hanbali* scholar, at an early age and then continued his studies in Mecca and Medina. In Medina *al-Wahhab* became friendly with *Muhammed Hayya al-Sindhi*, another *Hanbali* scholar who was to have a great influence on the young man.

Of particular interest is *Hayya's* emphasis on *ijtihad* (independent reasoning based on the Qur'an and *hadith*), a doctrine that he passed on to *al-Wahhab*. Strictly speaking only those scholars with sufficient knowledge and expertise in *jurisprudence* are qualified to practice *ijtihad*. Today, however, we are seeing individuals who are associated with some of the radical groups who claim to be practicing their own *itjihad* while their qualifications to do so will be extremely suspect.

Al-Wahhab also spent some time in Basrah, modern Iraq. Here he encountered many *Shi'a* whose beliefs and practices differed widely from his own. He was particularly disturbed by grave visitations and it is thought that this was the time that he began to formulate his own strong views against any kind of religious 'innovation'.

Muhammad Dawud Currie, in his paper *Kadizadeli Ottoman Scholarship, Muhammad Ibn Abdul-Wahhab and the rise of the Saudi State* dated June 2014, suggests that *al-Wahhab* might also have been influenced by the *Kadizadeli* movement of the Ottoman Empire.

The origins of the *Kadizadeli* can be traced back to *Imam Birgivi* (1522-1573) who was a respected scholar at the height of the Ottoman Empire. The movement actually takes its name from *Kadizade Mehmed Efendi* (1582-1635) who was a follower of *Birgivi* and admirer of *Ibn Taymiyya*. The *Kadizade* became extremely powerful under the patronage of Sultan Murad IV but they went into decline following the disastrous defeat of the Ottomans at the Battle of Vienna in 1683.

After the defeat of 1683 the *Kadizade* lost their patronage and many went into exile taking their reformist views with them. Consequently *Kadizade* influence, which was in many ways a continuation of *Hanbali* and *Ibn Taymiyya* thinking, spread as far as India and North Africa as well as Mecca and Medina. From Mecca elements of *Kadizade* thinking spread around the Muslim world via the pilgrim routes travelled by hundreds of thousands of Muslims who visited the holy city for the annual *Hajj*.

Some *Kadizade* found their way to Damascus and took up preaching and teaching posts at the famous *Umayyad* mosque. A number of these same scholars tutored *al-Wahhab*. According to Currie it is possible that the *Kadizade*, which prospered for so long in the Ottoman Empire, later influenced *al-Wahhab* who in turn promoted a *Muwahhdin* ideology that continues to this day.

Ibn Abdul Wahhab and Muhammad bin Saud

Al-Wahhab's reformist ideas were not universally accepted in his hometown of Uyayna. For example, he upset many when he levelled the grave of *Zayd ibn al-Khattab,* a respected companion of the Prophet, and his personal involvement in the stoning of a woman accused of adultery was condemned for its brutality. He was finally forced to leave the town.

He was then invited to settle in the nearby town of Diriyah by its ruler *Muhammad bin Saud*, an event that was to have monumental consequences for the world of Islam. An agreement was reached between the two men whereby together they would rid the Arabian Peninsula of all un-Islamic practices and restore the land to the 'true' faith. Under the terms of an oath, *al-Wahhab* would be responsible for all religious matters and *ibn Saud* for all political and military issues. A key element of their agreement was a commitment to *jihad* interpreted as the struggle to spread Islam. By way of further sealing the contract the ruler's son, *Abdul-Aziz bin Muhammad* married the daughter of *al-Wahhab* creating a family link that continues to this day.

By 1805 the *Wahhabi/Saud* partnership had destroyed the *Shi'a Imam Husayn Shrine* in Karbala, modern Iraq; they were in control of the holy cities of Mecca and Medina, which were officially under the rule of the Ottomans. For the next hundred years there was a power struggle for control over the Peninsula between the Ottomans, the Saudis and various Arab tribes.

With the help of the *Ikhwan*, a *Wahhabi* inspired religious militia, the Saudis finally managed to bring almost the entire Peninsula under its rule. In 1932, fourteen years after the dissolution of the Ottoman Empire, the Kingdom of Saudi Arabia was established with *Abd al-Aziz Al Saud,* better known as Ibn Saud as the nation's first King. In 1938 oil was discovered, an event that changed the country's course of history forever.

With increasing oil revenues, Saudi Arabia was able to fund and support *madrassas* (Islamic schools) across the Muslim world together with the *Wahhabi, or Muwahhidin* brand of Islam. The *Ahl al-Hadith* and *Deobandi* movements in India were both influenced by *Wahhabi* doctrine and both organisations have benefitted from Saudi Arabian funding.

Conclusion

In this chapter we have traced the development of reformist thinking from *Ibn Hanbal* (780-855) to *Ibn Taymiyya* (1263-1328) through to *Al-Wahhab* (1703-1792).

The thread that is common to all is a commitment to monotheism known as *Muwahhidin.* This is expressed through a denunciation of all forms of religious innovation that would include grave visits and the worship of saints. All emphasise the importance of the Qur'an, the *Hadith* and the *Sunnah* over against the schools of jurisprudence.

Ibn Hanbal, Ibn Taymiya and *Al-Wahhab* were all influenced by their own particular historical context. In each case this affected their own theological thought that was then passed on in preaching, teaching and the written word. As we saw in Chapter One, *Ibn Hanbal* formed his reformist views in direct response to the rational and philosophical climate of the early *Abbasid* period.

Both *Ibn Taymiyya* and *Al-Wahhab* were born into families of *Hanbali* scholars. *Ibn Taymiyya's* early life was influenced by the Mongol threat, the Crusader presence and what he perceived to be the weak faith of the *Mamluks.* It was in response to the Mongols in particular that he developed and refined his doctrine of the *jihad* as an armed struggle that was incumbent upon all Muslims. *Al-Wahhab* studied in Mecca and Medina and spent some time in Basrah where he encountered what he considered to be the heresies of the *Shi'a*. At one time the *Hanbali* scholar *Muhammad Hayya al-Sindhi* tutored *Al-Wahhab* and encouraged his student in *itjihad* (independent reasoning), a practice that would be adopted by later radical Islamist groups.

Crucially, *Al-Wahhab* lived at a time when parts of the Muslim world and the Arabian Peninsula in particular, were rebelling against the suzerainty of the Ottomans. This resulted in instability among the Arab tribes as each vied for power. It was in this context that *Al-Wahhab* and *Muhammad bin Saud* came together under oath, each committed to spread 'pure' Islam across the Peninsula; one by the power of religion and the other by the power of the sword.

The *Wahhabi/Saud* partnership continues to this day. However, with the backing of oil wealth and the recent patronage of the United States it has become far more powerful and its influence has spread well beyond the Arabian Peninsula.

CHAPTER FOUR

The Challenge of Arab Nationalism

Introduction

Arab nationalism, whereby the aim was unity on the basis of Arab identity and the Arabic language, drew people from different Arab states and across the religious divide, including many Christians, towards a common cause. 'Islamism' calls for unity based on the beliefs and values of Islam and therefore by definition would appeal only to Muslims.

The question of Arab Nationalism may not at first sight seem central to the theme of this book. However, there is no doubt that it has played its part in the growth of militant Islam and it has fed into the narrative of radical Islamism. In some ways Arab Nationalism, which surfaced around the middle of the 19th century and declined after the Six-Day war of 1967 between Israel and the Arab nations, was the precursor to the Islamism that is current today. For this reason it is important to look at the historical context that gave rise to Arab nationalism in the first place.

The Decline of Islamic Empires

For centuries of Islamic history the majority of Muslims in the world lived within three major Islamic Empires: the Ottoman Empire, the Mughal Empire and the Persian Empire. At its greatest extent, in 1683, the Ottoman Empire included large swathes of Europe, the Near East, North Africa and Arabia. After the First World War when the Empire was dissolved, all that remained was the modern state of Turkey that was founded in 1923. Most of the remaining Muslim lands of the Levant and North Africa that had previously been part of the Ottoman Empire found themselves under European rule.

In India the Mughal Empire, which had been in power since 1526, collapsed following the 'Indian Uprising' in 1857 when the last Mughal Emperor, Bahadur Shah II, was deposed and put under house arrest where he later died. The country then came under

British rule until it won its independence in 1947, becoming a republic in 1950.

Of particular significance was the forming of an international border in 1894 that separated British India from Afghanistan. The aim was to make Afghanistan a buffer zone between Russian and British interests. Known as the Durand Line after Sir Mortimer Durand, who was a British diplomat and civil servant, the 'line' was arbitrarily drawn through Pashtun tribal areas and the region of Balochistan. This resulted in the Pashtuns, the Baloch people and other ethnic groups being divided, with people from the same ethnic group or tribe being artificially separated and finding themselves in either Afghanistan or British India. In 1947 when both India and Pakistan won independence from the British, the line remained the same and Pakistan inherited the Eastern side of the international border.

Internationally, the Durand Line is still recognised as the border between Afghanistan and Pakistan. However, while the Pakistan Government officially accepts the border, Afghan tribes and especially the Pashtuns, who live on both sides of the boundary have never recognised its legality. Consequently the border between Pakistan and Afghanistan is both porous and dangerous. This goes some way to explaining why Pakistan has often been accused of harbouring terrorists based in Afghanistan such as Osama Bin Laden and the Taliban, both of which will be discussed in later chapters.

The Persian Empire, which was ruled by various Islamic dynasties and monarchies from the 7th century until the Islamic Revolution in 1979, has never been ruled by a European power but has nevertheless been affected by Western interference. A good example would be the abdication of *Reza Shah Pahlavi* in 1941 under pressure from the European allies and the subsequent replacement of his son *Mohammad Reza Shah Pahlavi*, a ruler who was much more likely to be compliant with Western interests.

Further interference occurred in 1953 when the democratically elected Iranian Prime Minister *Mosaddegh* was forced out of office at the instigation of the American CIA and British MI6. This was because the United States and Britain were unhappy about the fact that *Mosaddegh* had decided to nationalise Iranian oil.

For most Muslim societies the transition from an Islamic government to European rule was not easy, partly because many of the traditional forms of local government that had existed under the Ottomans were disbanded. It was in the context of disaffection with foreign rule and foreign interference that the beginnings of Arab nationalism took root.

While the largely Christian Balkan states, with support from Europe, gained independence from the Ottomans during the 19th century, the situation for the countries of the Levant and North Africa was different. These countries were simply calling for equal rights and more autonomy under the current regime rather than full independence from foreign rule, whether from the Ottomans or the Europeans.

The Ottoman Empire

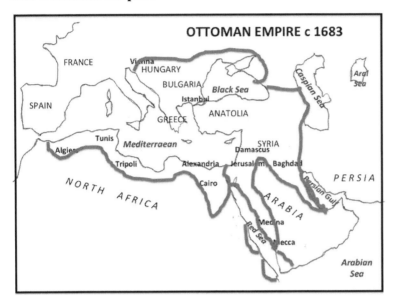

The defeat of the Ottomans at the walls of Vienna in 1683 marked the beginning of a very long and slow decline in Ottoman power. This was mirrored by an increase in European economic power due to industrialisation and the opening up of new sea routes to colonial markets, particularly those in the East Indies.

Beginning in the late 18th century both the Habsburg Empire, ruling central Europe from Vienna, and the rising Russian Empire, took advantage of Ottoman weakness in the Balkans. Both powers had territorial ambitions in the region and encouraged the Christian populations in the Balkan states to rise against their Islamic 'masters'.

In 1808 the Serbs revolted against the local Ottoman government and eventually, with European help, an autonomous Serbian state was established in 1830. Perhaps even more important was the Greek rebellion against the Ottomans that led to the Greek War of Independence (1821-1832) and finally the creation of an independent Greek Kingdom in 1833.

In North Africa the French occupied Algiers in 1830 and during the second half of the 19th century both France and Spain competed for control over Morocco. Italy ruled Libya between 1911 and 1927. In the Arabian Peninsula Aden was occupied by the British in 1839 and the Trucial States (Abu Dhabi, Dubai and Sharja) became a British Protectorate in 1853.

By 1914 and the outbreak of World War I the territory ruled by the Ottoman Empire, then known as 'the Sick Man of Europe', had been reduced to little more than a tiny piece of Europe surrounding Istanbul, most of Anatolia, the Levant and small coastal areas of the Arabian Peninsula.

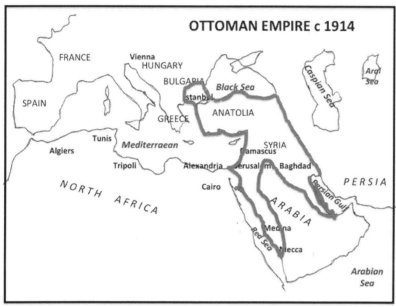

Aftermath of World War I

The Ottomans allied with the Central Powers (Germany, Austria-Hungary and Bulgaria) during World War I. As part of British strategy the Arab tribes of the Hejaz were encouraged to rebel against their Ottoman rulers. In what became known as the Arab Revolt of 1916-1918, the Arab ruler Sherif Hussein bin Ali, with support from the British Captain T E Lawrence (Lawrence of Arabia) joined forces with the British and French. The Arabs joined the allies on the understanding that should the Ottomans be defeated then an independent Arab state stretching from Aleppo in Syria down to Yemen would be established.

47

Unknown to many at the time, secret negotiations had been taking place between the British representative, Sir Mark Sykes, and the French diplomat, Francois Georges Picot concerning how best to define the different spheres of interest (British, French Russian) should the allies be victorious over the Ottomans. This became known as the *Sykes-Picot Agreement* or the *Asia Minor Agreement.* It was signed on 16 May 1916 and would signify the end of any hope of Arab independence as envisaged by the Arab rulers of the Hejaz.

The so-called Islamic State (IS) is now aiming to reverse the effects of the *Sykes-Picot Agreement.* In July 2014, in a speech at the Great Mosque at Mosul, the self-proclaimed Caliph *Abu Bakr Al-Baghdadi* said that the IS advance would not stop until the last nail in the coffin of the *Sykes-Picot Agreement* was hit.

Finding themselves on the losing side after the war, the Ottomans became signatories to the Treaty of Sevres that was signed in August, 1920. This marked the end of the era of World War I and the beginning of the official partition of the Ottoman Empire.

The terms of the Treaty were particularly harsh on the Ottomans. Of interest to us is the loss of Ottoman territory in the Levant that was arbitrarily divided up and mandated to Britain and France according to the *Sykes-Picot Agreement.*

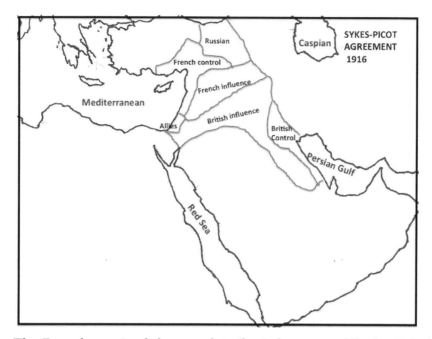

The French received the mandate for Lebanon and Syria. Britain was given the mandate for Iraq, known as the 'State of Iraq' and it placed King Faisal, a *Hashemite* (a descendant of the clan of the Prophet) as its client ruler. The British also put Sunni Arab elites into key positions of authority within the Iraqi government. This resulted in a minority Sunni establishment governing a majority Shi'a population, a situation that was unpopular among the majority *Shi'a.*

This balance of power between the *Sunni* and *Shi'a* continued until the downfall of Saddam Hussein (a *Sunni/Ba'athist*) in 2003 at the hands of the US led coalition, since which time a *Shi'a* dominated government has ruled. However sectarian conflicts in Iraq have continued resulting in political instability that has enabled both *Al-Qaeda* and ISIS to gain a foothold in the country.

Israel-Palestine

Under the Treaty of Sevres Britain received the mandate for Palestine, which from 1922 included Transjordan. The Treaty included the controversial 'Balfour Declaration' which was a letter dated 2 November 1917 written by the United Kingdom's Foreign Secretary Arthur James Balfour to the Second Baron

Rothschild who was then the first Jewish peer in England. The text of the letter, which was published later in the press, stated:

'His Majesty's government view with favour the establishment in Palestine of a national home for the Jewish people, and will use their best endeavours to facilitate the achievement of this object, it being clearly understood that nothing shall be done which may prejudice the civil and religious rights of existing non-Jewish communities in Palestine, or the rights and political status enjoyed by Jews in any other country'.

Pressure to provide the Jews with a homeland of their own grew following World War II and the tragedy of the Holocaust. When Britain terminated the mandate in 1947 the United Nations General Assembly adopted a resolution proposing the partition of Palestine into an Arab State and a Jewish State with Jerusalem coming under special international jurisdiction. While the Jews accepted the proposal the Arabs rejected it, which is not surprising since they had most to lose.

Stalemate led to civil war followed by the Declaration of the State of Israel in 1948. 700,000 Palestinians either fled or were driven from their homes and ended up as refugees in the neighbouring countries of Jordan and Lebanon. Over the following few years approximately 700,000 Jews, some of whom previously lived in Arab countries, entered Israel.

The Palestinians were denied the right of return to their homes and consequently large numbers remain in refugee camps to this day, particularly in Lebanon. This situation is just one of the many issues that the Arab and Muslim world finds unacceptable.

The Declaration of the State of Israel led to the 1948 Arab-Israeli war between Israel and the Arab League, which at that time included Egypt, Iraq, Jordan, Lebanon, Saudi Arabia and Syria. Israel defeated the Arab League and in the process seized a further 20 per cent of Palestinian land. A further Arab-Israeli war, lasting just six days, followed in 1967. On the Arab side the belligerents remained the same minus Saudi Arabia. However many countries of the Islamic world supported the war effort against the Israelis. Once again Israel, with its superior weaponry, defeated the allied Arab armies and seized further Palestinian territory. At this point Israel began its policy of building Jewish settlements, many being on land occupied by Palestinians.

Conflict has continued over the issue of Jewish settlements, the Palestinian right of return and the status of Jerusalem. The bombardment of Gaza by Israel in August 2014 has only increased resentment and anger across the Muslim world, once more feeding into the radical Islamist agenda.

Egypt

British interference in Egypt before the outbreak of World War I had resulted in a *de facto* British Protectorate that was formalised in 1914 with the installation of Hussain Kamel as Sultan. Protests against British rule came from the *Wafd* (Nationalist) Party and reached its peak following the exile of its leader *Saad Zaghlul* to Malta in March 1919. This, along with wartime deprivations imposed by the British due to World War I, led to Egypt's first modern revolution in 1919 and eventual independence from Britain on 28 February 1922.

The Egyptian monarchy was overthrown in 1952 and Gamal Abdel Nasser, a staunch supporter of both Arab and Egyptian nationalism, came to power. Nasser saw himself as leader of the Arab world over and against Israel and the Western powers. Nasser's successors Anwar Sadat and Hosni Mubarak were more interested in Egyptian nationalism than Arab nationalism. However, they both continued Nasser's focus on a secular Egypt rather than engage in the idea of an Islamic state.

It was in the context of Egypt's newfound independence that Egyptian schoolteacher, *Hassan-al-Banna* founded the Muslim Brotherhood, an Islamist social and political movement, in 1928. Concerned about the growth of secularism and Western influence, *Al-Banna* sought a return to Islamic values. The Muslim Brotherhood, which has subsequently spread to many other Muslim countries, will be discussed in later chapters.

Conclusion

By the middle of the 19th century the British had overthrown the Mughal Empire of India and the Ottoman Empire was in rapid decline, largely due to its inability to keep pace with the industrialisation and technology of Europe. In the other major Islamic Empire of Persia, Western interference was on the increase, a situation that would eventually lead to the Islamic Revolution in 1979.

The final collapse of the Ottoman Empire after World War I was as traumatic for the Islamic world as was the Fall of Constantinople in 1453 for the Christian world. In fact it was possibly even more so because it marked the end of the Caliphate.

Strictly speaking, as mentioned earlier, there can only be one Caliphate in Islam and even though Istanbul had little control over large parts of its Empire by the 19ᵗʰ century, it still held an important symbolic significance. In many ways, the dissolution of the Ottoman Empire resulted in a loss of central 'authority', even if only symbolic authority. This led to a psychological power vacuum that has resulted in both a loss of confidence within the Muslim world and also the proliferation of numerous Arab Nationalist and Islamist groups.

It is significant however that since the IS declaration of its 'Caliphate' there has been an increase around the Muslim world in the prospect of restoring the Caliphate. The concept of a revived Caliphate has always formed part of minority Islamic thinking but it is now being openly promoted and is drawing young Muslims from many European countries.

Al Monitor, the on-line Media Agency that monitors the Middle East, stated on 10 November 2014 that there has been an increase among young Muslims in Turkey who are supportive of IS and the 'Caliphate'. It has even been suggested that a Turkish (Ottoman) Caliphate, under President *Recep Tayyip Erdogan*, which would be Turkish rather than Arab, should be restored. *Boko Haram* in Nigeria is also calling for a Caliphate in Africa.

Some Muslims believe that the Islamic conquests of the early period were successful because the *Ummah* was following the will of God and that the rulers governed according to the Qur'an and early *hadith*. They now interpret the decline in Islamic power, often to the point of humiliation, as a consequence of the despotic and un-Islamic rule of its leaders, many of whom they regard as simply puppets of the West. Islamist groups such as IS, the *Taliban* and *Boko Haram* would take this view, claiming that the only answer for Muslims is to return to the 'pure' Islam of the first generations who lived under a Caliphate according to *Sharia* Law.

The various Arab nationalist groups that emerged in the 19th century tried to redress the balance between the Arab world and the West by calling for greater autonomy. Their hopes for independent rule were dashed following the secret *Sykes-Picot Agreement* and the final nail in the coffin of Arab nationalism was the humiliating defeat by the Israelis following the 1967 Six Day War.

As dreams of pan-Arab nationalism declined after 1967, some states, such as Egypt, Syria and Iraq focussed on their own secular nationalist agenda. In December 2010 a series of riots broke out in Tunisia following the suicide of a young man who was protesting about unemployment. This was the beginning of the Arab Spring, a series of uprisings in Egypt, Libya, Yemen, Syria and Bahrain, all of which, after initial euphoria, have resulted in increased instability. For different reasons both Iraq and Afghanistan, which will be discussed later, remain unstable.

With so much instability across the Muslim world Islamism has been able to flourish. It offers a renewed sense of purpose and hope for the many young Muslims who feel a deep sense of injustice, plus hypocrisy and betrayal by both the West and their own Islamic leaders.

CHAPTER FIVE

The Rise of Islamism

Introduction

The previous chapter explained how Pan-Arab and Arab nationalism rose in the context of the fall of the Ottoman Empire. When nationalism failed to address the problems facing the Arab Muslim world, many Muslims looked to their religion for the answer. In other words Islam became the foundation of political thought, a concept that is described as Political Islam or Islamism.

In this chapter we will look at two quite different examples of Islamist movements: first, the Muslim Brotherhood that was founded in Egypt in 1928 in the context of British rule and second, the *Taliban* that has its roots in the Soviet-Afghan war of 1979.

The term Islamism has frequently been used synonymously with Islamic fundamentalism in a derogatory way. But this is to confuse terms; Islamism is a political movement whereas Islamic fundamentalism is used to describe a conservative approach to the religion of Islam that is based on a literalist view of the Qur'an.

It is also important to differentiate between Islamic and Islamism. The former is descriptive, describing a religion and culture as Islamic, while Islamism refers to the political values and systems that are based on the religion of Islam.

Most Islamist groups follow a political agenda that is focussed on social and political reform that is compatible with Islam. These groups may, or may not be militant, but all take the view that there is no contradiction between Islamic values and Western modernisation and technology. An example would be a group such as ISIS that holds an extremely conservative view of Islam while at the same time uses sophisticated weaponry and modern communications systems.

An early advocate of Islamism was *Jamal ad-Din al-Afghani* (1830-1897), an Iranian political activist who promoted the adoption of modern Western technology in order to challenge increasing Western influence. *Al-Afghani's* ideas then informed the writing of Egyptian *Muhammad 'Abduh* (1849-1905). Both *al-Afghani* and *Muhammad 'Abduh* have had a lasting impact across the Muslim world.

Jamal ad-Din al-Afghani (1838/39 - 1897)

Al-Afghani was born in a small village near Hamadan, North West Iran. His family claimed the title of *sayyid* (descendants of the Prophet Muhammad through his grandsons *Hasan ibn Ali* and *Husayn ibn Ali*). Although *al-Afghani* was a *Shi'a* and was influenced by Iranian philosophers such as *Ibn Sina* (Avicenna), for much of his life he identified himself as an Afghan *Sunni.* He placed great emphasis on the need for rational thinking and was probably less concerned with the theological differences that separate *Sunni* and *Shi'a*. He was however passionate about political unity across the Muslim world.

When *al-Afghani* was about 17 years old he went to India where he spent several years studying religion. His time in India coincided with the Indian Uprising against the British in 1857-1858, an event that profoundly affected his political views regarding imperialism.

From India he went on pilgrimage to Mecca and then spent some years in Afghanistan where he was adviser to King *Dost Mohammed Khan* who reigned from 1826-1839 and from 1845-1863. This was a time when Afghanistan was caught up in the 'Great Game', a power struggle between Russia and Great Britain over access to India. With the change in monarchy following *Dost Mohammad Khan's* death, *al-Afghani* was forced into exile.

From Afghanistan he went to Egypt where he began teaching his ideas on political reform at the *al-Azhar* University in Cairo. One of his students was *Muhammad 'Abduh* (1849-1905) who was later to become the *Mufti* (scholar in Islamic law) of Egypt. *Muhammad 'Abduh* came from a strict *Hanbali* (see Chapter One) family but he also believed in independence of thought and the importance of reason and he was passionate about the need to provide an education that equipped Muslims for the modern world.

In 1878, *al-Afghani* was exiled because of his radical views and *Muhammad 'Abduh* was forced to return to his hometown.

After Egypt, *al-Afghani* spent time in Istanbul, Moscow and various European cities including London and Paris. He also returned to Iran for a short time and he was openly critical of *Shah Nasser ad-Din's* policy of granting generous trade concessions to Britain at the expense of Iranians.

Al-Afghani's political views were formed against the context of his own experiences in India, Afghanistan, Egypt and Iran. He was disappointed at the failure of the Indian Uprising. He felt that Afghanistan was a political pawn at the hands of the British and the Russians. He was disturbed by British influence in both Egypt and Iran. Consequently, he became extremely suspicious of European imperialism believing it to be a threat to the Middle East.

His solution to European imperialism was to embrace the best of Western technology and also adopt modernism as long as this was not in conflict with Islamic values. His strategy was to encourage the mobilisation of the people through his preaching that modernism and traditional Islamic values are compatible. In other words, he preached political Islam or Islamism.

Al-Afghani's anti-imperialism was to have a profound effect not only on *Muhammad 'Abduh,* but also on *Muhammad Rashid Rida* (1865-1935). Both scholars were then to influence the thinking of *Hasan al-Banna*, founder of Egypt's Muslim Brotherhood.

Muslim Brotherhood

The Society of Muslim Brothers, better known as the Muslim Brotherhood, was founded in Egypt in 1928 by *Hasan al-Banna* (1906-1949) who was an Islamic scholar and schoolteacher. *Al-Banna* was brought up in a pious home, his father being a respected *Hanbali* imam and he was also interested in Sufism and the writings of *Rashid Rida,* referred to above.

Al-Banna became politically aware at the age of 17 as a result of the Egyptian Revolution against British occupation in 1919. In 1927, following his studies, he took up a post as a primary school teacher in the town of Ismailia. The town is situated on the West bank of the Suez Canal and in 1927 it was the headquarters of the Suez Canal Authority. As a result, Ismailia had a very large European population and *Al Banna* became concerned that their presence was having an unfavourable effect on the religion and culture of Egyptian Muslims in the region.

In March, 1928 *Al Banna* was approached by a small group of workers from the Suez Canal companies who complained to him about the poor treatment of Arabs and Muslims by their employers. *Al-Banna* took up their cause, so marking the founding in Egypt of the Muslim Brotherhood.

The early motto of the Brotherhood was 'Believers are but Brothers'. This later became: "Allah is our objective. The Prophet is our leader. The Qur'an is our law. *Jihad* is our way. Dying in the way of Allah is our highest hope Allahu akbar!" A more recent, and shorter motto is: "Islam is the solution".

By the end of the Second World War the Muslim Brotherhood had some two million members in branches across Egypt. From the beginning it combined political activism with a strong programme of social care, providing health clinics, sports facilities, schools, mosques and community centres. As a movement the Muslim Brotherhood has spread beyond Egypt into many other Muslim countries such as Jordan and the Palestinian territories of Gaza and the West Bank.

In some of these countries independent political organisations have been formed, but they are still affiliated to the Muslim Brotherhood in Egypt. Also many hundreds of individual members who live and work in Saudi Arabia and the Gulf States support the Muslim Brotherhood through regular financial donations.

A key thinker who was associated with the Muslim Brotherhood was Sayyid Qutb (1906-1966), who was a leading Islamic theorist as well as a prolific writer and poet. Qutb spent two years in the United States and it was this experience that led to his distaste of all things American, particularly its materialism, racism, sexual freedom and support for Israel. In 1966 he was accused of plotting the assassination of President Gamal Abdel Nasser, found guilty and executed by hanging. His thinking has continued to influence Islamists such as *Al-Qaeda* who are sometimes referred to as *Qutbists.*

Since its inception in Egypt in 1928, the Muslim Brotherhood has stressed the importance of social reform and has been extremely successful in founding hospitals, schools and even commercial projects. However, as it became more influential in society it gradually became more politically active. The organisation openly opposed British rule in 1936, supported the Arabs in the 1948 Arab-Israel war and backed the Egyptian Revolution of 1952. As a result of these political activities, the Brotherhood has at various times been suppressed, declared illegal and had hundreds of its members executed and imprisoned.

With the outbreak of the Arab Spring in 2011, and the fall of President Hosni Mubarak, the Muslim Brotherhood was declared legal after a long period in isolation. The organisation then formed the *Freedom and Justice Party* under the chairmanship of Mohamed Morsi who became Egypt's first democratically elected President in June 2012. A year later, in July 2013, President Morsi was deposed following riots and protests against allegations of misrule. Apart from discontent with his authoritarian style, many feared that Morsi's Islamist agenda would have been detrimental to liberal and secular groups in the country and especially religious minorities such as the Christian Copts.

Following Morsi's ousting at the hands of General Abdel Fattah el-Sisi, Head of the Egyptian Armed Forces, Muslim Brotherhood supporters staged protests and sit-ins across the country. The military cracked down heavily on the protesters, a state of emergency was declared, many lost their lives and hundreds were imprisoned. President Morsi was accused of inciting violence and was arrested.

In September, 2013 the organisation was once again declared illegal and had its assets seized. In March 2014 over 500 members of the Brotherhood were sentenced to death. Muhamed Morsi, at the time of writing, remains in custody awaiting trial and the Muslim Brotherhood has been declared a terrorist organisation by Egypt, and many other countries including Bahrain, Russia, Syria, Saudi Arabia and United Arab Emirates.

KEY RADICAL THINKERS

IBN HANBAL 780-855
Challenged liberalism of Abbasids

IBN TAYMIYYA 1263-1328
Developed theory of Jihad at time of Mongol invasions

AL-WAHHAB 1703-1792
Radical preacher joined forces with Al-Saud

AL-AFGHANI 1838-1897
Became anti-Imperial following Indian Mutiny

AL-BANNA 1906-1949
Influenced by Al-Afghani – founded Muslim Brotherhood

SAYYID QUTB 1906-1966
Member of Muslim Brotherhood – influenced Al-Qaeda

The Afghan Taliban - Background

Although the *Taliban* can also be described as an Islamist group on account of its political agenda, it differs from the Muslim Brotherhood in that it is also an Islamic fundamentalist movement that advocates a particularly conservative view of Islam. As a result it has been highly criticised by Muslim and non-Muslim countries for its uncompromising interpretation of *Sharia* Law and particularly its treatment of women.

The word *Taliban* means 'students' (plural of *talib* - student) in *Pashto,* the native language of the *Pashtun* people of South-Central Asia. In order to understand the *Taliban* it is helpful to look at the recent history of Afghanistan.

Some fourteen tribes or ethnic groups populate the country, the largest being the *Pashtun* (50%-60%) with the *Tajiks* as the second largest. The historical home of the *Pashtun* stretches from Afghanistan into North West Pakistan where they make up the second largest ethnic group of the region. As mentioned in the previous chapter, many *Pashtun* do not recognise the official boundary that splits their tribe between Afghanistan and Pakistan. As a result there are some *Pashtun* whose loyalty to the tribe takes priority over loyalty to the country, a situation that has been problematic for Pakistan.

For many centuries the country was fought over between the Persians in the West and various Turkic empires of the East. In the 19th century Afghanistan was caught up in the battle between Britain and Russia for control over trade routes to British India. Between 1839 and 1919, in its attempt to control Afghanistan and keep Russia at bay, Britain embarked upon three military expeditions known as the Anglo-Afghan wars, all of which were a disaster for the British.

In 1919, following the Third Anglo-Afghan War, Afghanistan was declared an independent and sovereign state under the monarchy of King *Amanullah Khan*. *King Amanullah* and his successor, King *Mohammed Zahir Shah* established diplomatic relations with the international community and introduced many reforms in an attempt to modernise and westernise the country. These included greater political freedom, co-educational schools and the abolition of the traditional burqa for women. Not surprisingly some of these reforms alienated the more traditional tribal Afghans.

In 1973 *Mohammed Daoud Khan*, cousin of King *Zahir Shah*, deposed the King in a bloodless coup and became the first President of the Republic of Afghanistan. President *Daoud Khan* favoured closer relations with the Soviets and his accession to power marked a significant moment in the history of Afghanistan.

The communist 'People's Democratic Party of Afghanistan' seized power in September 1979. This led to an uprising by those opposed to communist rule and when civil war eventually broke out between government forces and the *mujihadeen* (Islamic fighters/Jihadists), Soviet troops entered Afghanistan in order to stabilise the situation. The Soviets remained in Afghanistan for ten years during which time the country was ruled along communist lines with women being given greater equality.

However, Communism was not compatible with the more traditional Islamic and tribal values of the Afghan people and resistance grew under the *mujihadeen* resulting in a ten-year uprising against Soviet occupation. For strategic reasons Pakistan was keen to regain its influence in Afghanistan and so it supported the *mujihadeen* against the Soviets. Pakistan trained *jihadi* fighters and supplied weapons that were paid for by the United States and Saudi Arabia. During this period Pakistan's 'Inter-Services Intelligence' (ISI) forces trained some 90,000 Afghans, including *Mohammad Omar*, who later became leader of the Afghan *Taliban*.

United States' support for the *mujihadeen* has to be seen within the context of its relations with the Soviet Union during the Cold War. This was a period following the Secon World War, when political and military tension prevailed between the Western Bloc (the United States, NATO and their allies) and the Eastern Bloc (the Soviet Union and its allies).

The *mujihadeen* recruited fighters from across the Islamic world with a large number coming from Saudi Arabia. One such fighter was *Osama bin Laden* who will be discussed in the next chapter. Many of the *mujihadeen*, all of whom were supported by the United States and Saudi Arabia, were later to become leaders of the *Taliban.*

When the Soviet forces finally left Afghanistan in February 1989 the country was left to rule itself under the presidency of pro-Soviet *Mohammad Najibullah. Najibullah* was deposed in 1992 and very quickly the country fell into anarchy. War broke out between the various tribal and ethnic warlords who constantly switched sides and changed alliances as each jostled for power.

In the South, around Kandahar, much of the farming economy had already collapsed during the Soviet period. To add to the suffering of the people the warlords seized what was left of their homes and farms. Drug trafficking was rife. Kidnapping and all forms of atrocities were committed against the population and especially against young girls and boys. All this resulted in a further exodus of refugees, adding to those who had already left during the Soviet occupation. Most went to Pakistan only to swell the numbers already living in refugee camps and *madrassas*.

Mullah Mohammad Omar

Little is known about *Mohammad Omar*, usually referred to as *Mullah Omar*, other than that he came from a poor rural background in the Kandahar Province and fought with the *mujihadeen* against the Russians. After the withdrawal of the Soviets he returned to his previous occupation of teaching in a *madrassa*, first in Pakistan and then in Kandahar.

Along with many, he was shocked by the corruption and atrocities that he witnessed after the fall of *Najibullah*. It is reported that in the spring of 1994 he and a small band of 30 men with 16 rifles between them rescued two girls who had been captured by the warlords. Following another incident when he rescued a young boy from rape, people began calling on him for help. And so began the rise of the *Taliban*, so called because many of its recruits were students from the *madrassas* of Afghanistan and Pakistan.

Within months some 15,000 students had arrived from Pakistan to join *Mullah Omar* and by the end of the year the *Taliban* controlled not only Kandahar but also 12 out of 34 provinces. In September 1996 the *Taliban* founded the Islamic Emirate of Afghanistan with Kandahar as its capital and *Mullah Omar* as Head of State.

Taliban Ideology

The unstable situation in Afghanistan that started with the fall of King *Mohammed Zahir Shah* in 1973 and continued throughout the Soviet occupation, led to an exodus of refugees including many orphans, to Pakistan. The refugee camps were funded by Saudi Arabia, as were the *madrassas* where the orphans both lived and were educated.

The *Deobandi*, a conservative revivalist movement that was formed in the 19th century in the context of opposition to British rule in India, ran most of these *madrassas*. Consequently, the students inherited the conservative doctrine of the *Deobandi* with its fundamental aversion to foreign power. The students were also influenced by the *Wahhabi* doctrine of their financial patrons (see Chapter Three).

Most of the younger *Taliban* were born in the refugee camps in Pakistan and therefore had little or no knowledge of Afghanistan and its heritage. The orphans, who went to Pakistan as refugees, grew up in *madrassas* and had no experience of family life. Their contact with women was virtually non-existent and this goes some way to explain their later treatment of women in Afghanistan.

From the beginning *Mullah Omar* was seen as the champion of the people, as someone who stood up to the warlords. He, and those who joined him, believed that they were purging society from corruption and brutality. Their stated aims were to 'restore peace, disarm the population, enforce *Sharia* Law and defend the integrity and Islamic character of Afghanistan' (Ahmad Rashid, *Taliban*). Combined with a strict adherence to the *Sharia* Law, the *Taliban* also follow *Pashtunwali*, the traditional tribal code of the *Pashtun* people.

While most of the stated aims of the *Taliban* sound plausible, their particular interpretation of *Sharia* has been highly criticised as being un-Islamic. For example, the banning of music, dancing, television, sport and above all, education for girls is not supported by reference to the Qur'an or *Hadith*.

In relation to women the *Taliban* introduced particularly severe decrees. For example: '*Women you should not step outside your residence. If you go outside the house you should not be like women who used to go with fashionable clothes wearing much cosmetics and appearing in front of every men [sic] before the coming of Islam....if women are going outside with fashionable, ornamental, tight and charming clothes to show themselves, they will be cursed by the Islamic Sharia and should never expect to go to Heaven.'* (Decree announced by the Religious Police in Kabul 1996 quoted by Ahmad Rashid, *Taliban*)

In the early years the *Taliban* were welcomed by many as liberators who freed them from the tyranny of the warlords. Thousands of young men left the camps and *madrasses* to join *Mullah Omar* as well as *jihadists* from around the Muslim world. In time, however, the people began to resent the brutal, almost medieval regime of *Taliban* rule.

Taliban Post 9/11

Between 1996 and the attack on the Twin Towers on 11 September 2001 the *Taliban* consolidated their power with continued support from Pakistan and Saudi Arabia. During this same period the names of *Osama Bin Laden* and *Al Qaeda*, (see the following chapter) were increasingly heard in the world media in relation to terrorist attacks such as the 1998 United States Embassy bombings in Dar es Salaam and Nairobi.

The attack of 9/11 was attributed to *Bin Laden* who was thought at that time to be hiding in Afghanistan under the protection of the *Taliban* and with the full knowledge of Pakistan. On 15 September President George W Bush gave Pakistani President *Pervez Musharraf* an ultimatum demanding the handing over of *Bin Laden* with the words 'you are either with us or against us'. At this point Pakistan officially switched sides in support of the US and her allies in opposition to the *Taliban*. However, neither Pakistan nor the *Taliban* were prepared to hand over the accused terrorist.

On 7 October the US began bombing *Taliban* bases. By 5 December *Mullah Omar* was forced to surrender Kandahar and he escaped into the desert on a motorbike. At the time of writing he is still in hiding. The *Taliban* lost between 8,000 and 12,000 fighters but many, including its leaders, managed to escape into the Tora Bora Mountains or across the border into Pakistan's tribal areas.

Within weeks of defeating the *Taliban* the US turned its attention to Iraq. It left behind a country destroyed by decades of war, a wrecked economy, a broken infrastructure and the loss of a traditional tribal system that had sustained Afghan society for centuries. Crucially however, thousands of *Taliban*, including the leaders, had managed to escape.

The Pakistani Taliban (*Tehrik-i-Taliban* Pakistan)

Many of those who escaped the American invasion, including Arabs, Central Asians, Chechens and Africans, made their way to either Baluchistan in Pakistan or to the Federally Administered Tribal Areas (FATA), a semi-autonomous tribal region located in North West Pakistan.

FATA offered a safe haven for both Afghan *Taliban* and *Al Qaeda*. The region also provided an opportunity for the fighters to re-form. In December 2007 a number of tribal militias, including some from Punjab and Kashmir, joined forces to create the *Tehrik-i-Taliban* Pakistan (Pakistani *Taliban*).

While both the Afghan and Pakistani *Taliban* are predominantly *Pashtun* and share some similarities when it comes to ideology, there are differences in their history and stated aims. The Afghan *Taliban* are fighting a Western international coalition as well as the Afghan Government. The *Tehrik-i-Taliban* Pakistan, on the other hand, are fighting the Pakistani Government, its stated aims being: to oppose the Pakistani Government, to oppose UN forces in Afghanistan and to enforce its own interpretation of *Sharia* Law.

The December 2014 attack on the Military Public School in Peshawar that killed 141 people including 132 students was carried out by the Pakistani *Taliban* and is an example of the group's war against the Pakistani government and its forces. The attack was in retaliation for the military bombing of Pakistani *Taliban* bases in FATA that killed innocent civilians including many children.

The shooting of schoolgirl *Malala Yousafzai* in January 2009 by the same group is evidence of the Pakistani *Taliban*'s opposition to girls' education, a position they hold in common with the Afghan *Taliban.*

Conclusion

With the dissolution of the Ottoman Empire after the First World War most of the Arab Muslim world found itself under European rule with new national borders. In reaction to this situation, some Arab nations decided to focus on Arab identity as a way forward in uniting the people. When Arab or Pan-Arab nationalism, being political movements, failed there was a move towards seeing Islam as a uniting force. This is termed political Islam or Islamism.

One of the first proponents of Islamism was *Jamal ad-Din al-Afghani*, an Iranian Islamic scholar and political thinker. *Al-Afghani* strongly believed that if Muslims were to find their equal place alongside the West, then they needed to adopt modern Western technology. However, this should not be at the expense of undermining Islamic values. He further claimed that modernism and Islam are not mutually exclusive.

Al-Afghani was widely travelled. He was in India at the time of the Indian Uprising in 1857/1858, an experience that profoundly affected his attitude towards imperialism. When he later taught at *Al Azhar* University in Cairo he was to influence *Muhammad 'Abduh* and *Muhammad Rashid Rida.* Both of these scholars were then to influence *Hasan al-Banna*, founder of the Muslim Brotherhood in 1928.

The Muslim Brotherhood was formed in the context of Arab grievances against the Suez Canal Authority that was being run at the time by Europeans. From the beginning the Muslim Brotherhood was essentially a vehicle for social reform. It never subscribed to a particularly strong religious ideology. It did. However, become politicised and this is what led to it being banned by the Egyptian Government and declared a terrorist organisation. Consequently, many of its supporters have been executed, imprisoned or have gone into exile. Some have subsequently joined radical Islamist groups including IS.

The *Taliban,* in common with the Muslim Brotherhood, also has a political agenda but it differs in that its extreme interpretation of the *Sharia* underpins its ideology and its actions. Both organisations emerged at a time of political and social unrest. In both cases the founders responded to the needs of the people; *al-Banna* went to the aid of the employees of the Suez Canal Authority and *Mullah Omar* to the rescue of abused children. As a result, both *al-Banna* and *Mullah Omar* attracted a following that over time grew to many thousands.

The Muslim Brotherhood has spread beyond Egypt and has affiliates, both groups and individuals, in many other Arab countries while the *Taliban* has remained within the Afghanistan/Pakistan region. In 2007 a separate Pakistani *Taliban* was formed that holds to the same extreme interpretation of the *Sharia* as the Afghan *Taliban* but is working in open opposition to the Pakistan Government.

For different reasons both the Muslim Brotherhood and the *Taliban* have been declared terrorist organisations by various governments. One consequence of being illegal is that the members disperse and go underground. Many become disillusioned and join more radical groups.

While the *Taliban* has remained a regional organisation, early on in its history it attracted both foreign fighters and foreign money. Some of these foreign fighters have subsequently returned to their home countries taking with them the extremist ideology of the *Taliban*.

In the years preceding the attack on the Twin Towers in 2001, *Osama bin Laden* and a small group of followers who became known as *Al Qaeda*, took refuge with the *Taliban* in Afghanistan. This was to change the history of the *Taliban* in particular and the growth of militant Islam in general.

CHAPTER SIX

The emergence of Violent Extremism

In the summer of 2014 an unprecedented form of violent Islamic extremism erupted in the Middle East that shocked the world. Images of public beheadings appeared on our television screens together with reports of kidnapping, massacres and atrocities committed against innocent men, women and children. The perpetrators were members of a group calling itself ISIS (Islamic State of Iraq and Syria) or IS (Islamic State).

In order to understand how this came about it is necessary to go back to the origins of *Al-Qaeda* and the person of *Osama bin Laden* who is said to be the mind behind that organisation.

Osama bin Laden: early life (1957-1979)

Osama bin Laden was born in Riyadh, Saudi Arabia in March 1957. He was the seventeenth child of *Mohammed bin Awad bin Laden,* a self-made billionaire who was born in Yemen and made his fortune in the construction industry building roads, bridges and royal palaces in Saudi Arabia. *Bin Laden's* mother was from Syria and was an Alawite, which is a minority *Shi'a* Muslim sect that is considered heretical by most *Sunni* Muslims. President Assad of Syria and many of Syria's ruling elite are Alawite, a fact that contributes to the current civil war in Syria and Sunni opposition to the regime.

Those who knew *Osama bin Laden* claimed that he was quiet, well mannered and softly spoken with an excellent command of classical Arabic. Although none of his family adhered to the strict *Wahhibism* of Saudi Arabia (see Chapter Three) it is said that *Osama* had shown an interest in religion from a very early age. He was serious, prayed regularly, frequently attending the mosque and studying the Qur'an. He showed no interest in the usual teenage activities apart from football.

Bin Laden's parents were divorced soon after he was born and his mother remarried and had several more children. Although he lived with his mother, with whom he was very close, *Bin*

Laden's father continued to take a great interest in the boy, not only ensuring that he received a good education but also taking him on outings into the desert and later involving him in the family construction business.

This civil engineering experience was later to prove extremely useful to *Osama bin Laden.* After the attack on the Twin Towers in September 2001 he went into hiding from American forces in the *Toro Boro* mountains of Afghanistan. Using the skills he acquired from his father he was able to build a complex of tunnels, linking living quarters, first aid rooms and offices, deep into the caves so giving him almost foolproof cover.

Bin Laden married his first wife, who was from Syria like his mother, when he was 17. It is speculated that he had six wives in all, two of whom he divorced and he fathered 20 children. Although he inherited great wealth from his father he lived a frugal life. He was strict with his children and wanted his sons to experience the hardships of life just as he had learned from his own father. He taught them to ride, took them on shooting and hunting trips in the desert and he made sure that they could walk barefoot in the hot sand.

When *Mohammed bin Laden* died in a plane crash the family business passed to the elder sons who had all been educated in exclusive private schools and universities in the West. *Osama bin Laden* chose not to travel overseas for his education. Instead he attended King *Abdul Aziz* University in Jeddah where he studied economics and business administration.

During his time at university it is possible that his tutor might have been *Abdullah Yusuf Azzam*, a Palestinian from Jenin in the West Bank. *Azzam* was extremely intelligent and had studied *Sharia* Law at both the University of Damascus and the *Al-Azhar* University in Cairo before taking up a post in Jeddah. Significantly however he was a member of the Muslim Brotherhood. As mentioned in the previous chapter, the Brotherhood had established groups across the region and during the 1960s and 1970s Saudi Arabia welcomed many

Brotherhood refugees from Egypt and other Muslim countries as teachers in its universities.

As a member of the Muslim Brotherhood, *Azzam* had already imbibed the concept of political Islam through the writings of *Hasan Al-Banna* (see Chapter Five) and other Brotherhood thinkers. He then became even more radical in his outlook following the 1967 Six Day Arab-Israeli War when Israel occupied his home in the West Bank resulting in *Azzam* and his family joining the exodus of Palestinian refugees into Jordan.

By the time *Azzam* and *Osama bin Laden* were both at the King *Abdul Aziz* University in the late 1970s, *Azzam* was teaching a hardline view of militant *jihad* claiming it to be an obligatory duty of all Muslims. While there is some uncertainty as to whether or not the two men actually met in Jeddah in the 1970s, there is no doubt that they later became very close during the 1980s in Afghanistan.

The Significance of 1979

Three major events occurred in the Muslim world in 1979 that might at first glance appear to be unrelated. The first was the Iranian Revolution in **January** 1979. The second was the siege of the Grand Mosque in Mecca by a group of Islamist extremists in **November** 1979. This was an indirect consequence of the Iranian Revolution. The third event was the Soviet invasion of Afghanistan in **December** 1979 that was covered in the previous chapter. This latter event was to have repercussions across the Islamic world.

The Iranian Revolution is also referred to as the Islamic Revolution, reflecting the fact that the pro-Western Shah was overthrown by the people of Iran and replaced by an Islamic theocracy. This is covered in another book in the *In Brief Series: From the Medes to the Mullahs: a History of Iran.*

The success of the Iranian Revolution stirred up discontent in other Muslim countries, Saudi Arabia being one. On 20 November 1979 a group of some 400 extremists, led by *Juhayman al-Otaybi,* a militant activist who was opposed to the monarchy, seized the Grand Mosque in Mecca, the most holy site in Islam. Hundreds of pilgrims were either made hostages or killed in crossfire. The protestors were calling for the overthrow of the House of Saud, which they considered corrupt and un-Islamic, and replacement by the *Mahdi* (a saviour figure). They further claimed that the *Mahdi* was the brother-in- law of *al-Otaybi* who, according to them, was expected to appear on 20 November 1979, the very day of the siege.

The siege lasted two weeks and was finally brought to an end by the Saudi army with the help of French forces. *Al-Otaybi* and 63 militants were executed by public beheading in cities across the Kingdom.

The reaction of the monarchy was to introduce even more severe religious laws in the form of strict *Wahhabism*. In order to enforce conformity, greater power was given to the *Ulema* and religious police. The outcome was that in 1979 Saudi Arabia entered a period of increased religious conservatism just at a time when many of its citizens were to travel to Afghanistan.

The third event of significance for the Muslim world in 1979 was the Soviet invasion of Afghanistan that occurred in the December, just one month after the humiliation of the mosque siege. The Saudis immediately took up the cause of their Muslim brothers in Afghanistan by declaring *jihad* against the 'infidel' Soviet invaders.

In mosques across the country preachers spoke of the plight of Afghanistan. Young men were encouraged join the fight in defense of Islam just as Muslims had done 800 years previously against the Western crusaders.

To some extent embarking on the Afghan *jihad* in the name of Islam was a way for the monarchy to restore its reputation, which had been so besmirched the previous month. Equally important was that it presented an opportunity to get rid of those radical elements that threatened the stability of the Kingdom. This latter point also applied to many other Muslim countries, from North Africa to SE Asia, all of whom supported the Afghan *jihad*.

Osama bin Laden and the Soviet War in Afghanistan

The Saudi monarchy and wealthy individuals raised money in support of both the volunteers who went to fight and also the Afghan refugees who had fled to Pakistan. Just a few years into the war *Osama bin Laden,* being a young wealthy Saudi, was asked to join the fundraising efforts. His role took him to Afghanistan where he stayed with none other than *Abdullah Yusuf Azzam,* the radical Palestinian who had taught at King *Abdul Aziz* University. This was to be the beginning of a close relationship between the two.

The two men established an office in a quiet suburb of Peshawar, Pakistan and also a hostel to accommodate the arriving volunteers and those returning from Afghanistan. Apart from fundraising, *bin Laden* frequently crossed the border into Afghanistan where he visited the soldiers. He took a special interest in the wounded and it is said that he gave out chocolates and took down the names and addresses of families ensuring that he would pass on news and money to those at home. He became extremely popular and his reputation spread across the Islamic world as both a role model and religious icon.

When the tide began to turn against the Soviets, *bin Laden*, *Azzam* and their associates started thinking about taking *jihad* beyond Afghanistan into the global arena. *Azzam* was still committed to the ideology of the Muslim Brotherhood and preferred to recruit volunteers from a narrow stratum of the more educated and elite of Muslim society. *Bin Laden*, on the other hand, had moved away from the Brotherhood and was prepared to accept Muslims of any background, ethnicity, rich, poor and even those with a criminal background. Regardless of ethnicity, they were all known as 'Afghan Arabs'.

While *Azzam* believed that the volunteers should fight alongside the Afghans, *bin Laden* wanted his volunteers to fight as a separate unit. It was around this time, in 1988, that a formal group was set up with the name *al-Qaeda,* meaning 'the Base', although the name was not at that time used publicly.

Osama bin Laden: from Hero to Exile: 1989-1992

When the Soviets finally left Afghanistan in February 1989 a few of *bin Laden's* volunteers remained and married Afghan women. However, the majority of the Arab Afghans returned to their home countries where they were viewed with some caution partly due to their background as militants but also because they had been exposed to the extreme *Wahhabism* of the Saudi volunteers.

Bin Laden was initially welcomed by the Saudi monarchy as a war hero and he was *fêted* wherever he went. This adulation reinforced his sense of invincibility and his commitment to defend Islam and Muslims wherever they were under oppression. He spoke passionately about the plight of the Palestinians, the Chechens and also the Bosnians during the Yugoslav wars between 1991 and 1999.

Another cause that he felt strongly about was the virtual civil war that raged in Yemen, his father's homeland. His outspokenness and financial support for *jihadists* in Yemen annoyed the Saudi monarchy. Since Yemen was its Southern neighbour and extremely volatile, the Saudis treated the country with caution and did not want a young firebrand meddling in the Kingdom's foreign affairs.

Relations between *bin Laden* and the monarchy came to crisis point in 1990 when Saddam Hussein invaded Kuwait. Despite being extremely wealthy, Saudi Arabia did not have the military expertise to defend itself against a potential Iraqi invasion. *Bin Laden* immediately offered his services to both liberate Kuwait and defend the Kingdom with his army of Afghan veterans who were both well-armed and well-trained.

He was rebuffed and his offer rejected. Instead the monarchy accepted the protection of the United States and American forces soon had boots on the ground in 'the Land of the Two Holy Mosques'. At the time it was agreed that the US forces would leave once Kuwait was liberated. To the anger of many Saudis the Americans remained until 2003 when most were withdrawn, leaving behind a few small training units.

The presence of 'infidels' in the land of the Prophet angered the more conservative Saudis. *Osama bin Laden* had always been critical of the monarchy for its corruption and despotism but above all he accused it of being a puppet of America. 1990 was to be the turning point. This was the moment when the United States became the great enemy of *bin Laden.* He now declared that *jihad* against America and her allies, particularly Israel and the United Kingdom, was not only justified but obligatory.

By 1992 the relationship between *bin Laden* and the monarchy had finally broken down and he was banished from the Kingdom and stripped of his citizenship. He then moved to Sudan where he established a new base for *al-Qaeda* and built closer links with Egyptian Islamic Jihad (EIJ). In 1996, under increasing pressure from the United States, Egypt and Saudi Arabia, Sudan finally expelled both the EIJ and *bin Laden.* He was offered transport and a choice of destination. He chose to return to Afghanistan. On 8 May 1996 he boarded a chartered plan with 300 Afghan Arabs bound for Jalalabad in Eastern Pakistan.

Al-Qaeda in Afghanistan 1996-2001

Once back in Afghanistan *bin Laden* set about organising training camps and seeking recruits. He also invited other active militant groups such as *Hamas* and *Hezbollah* to join his network. Both declined on the grounds that they had their own regional agenda.

Al-*Qaeda* in Afghanistan offered aspiring militants a range of services that can broadly be divided into three: a) financial aid to cover the cost of travel to training camps or for the purchase of munitions; b) advice on such things as assassinations and bomb making; c) hands-on terrorist training.

Al-Qaeda was never a structured organisation with a hierarchy of command. However after *bin Laden* returned to Afghanistan in 1996 the group did establish a system of operation that had three essential elements. Jason Burke, in his book *Al-Qaeda; the True Story of Radical Islam*, describes these elements as 'a hardcore, a network of co-opted groups and an ideology'.

The hardcore consisted of *bin Laden* and some twenty to thirty close associates, some of whom were veterans of the Afghan-Soviet War and others key militants from across the globe. The hardcore acted as trainers and administrators and occasionally travelled around the world on funding and recruitment campaigns.

There was no formal agreement between the hardcore and the groups that made up the network. Equally there were no formal links between the groups or cells. The network was, and still is, extremely fluid with groups changing their name and members moving from one group or cell to another at will. This is the current situation in Syria where the fighters will move between the various factions opposing President Assad's government forces and those who are fighting ISIS.

The only thing that was, and is, common to all, whether the hardcore or the network, is the third element, the ideology that over time has developed into what could be described as an *al-Qaeda* worldview. And it is this same worldview that drives the countless groups of militant Islamists that exist today.

Al-Qaeda Post 9/11

As mentioned in the previous chapter, *Al-Qaeda* was suspected of the bombings in 1998 of the United States Embassies in Dar es Salaam and Nairobi. Following the attack on the Twin Towers on 11 September 2001 *Bin Laden* was the key suspect. The Bush administration offered a reward of $25 million for any information leading to his capture or death.

Since he was thought at that time to be hiding in Afghanistan under the protection of the *Taliban,* United States and Afghan forces embarked upon a military campaign in Afghanistan's *Toro Boro* Mountains in an attempt to find him. Hundreds of *Al-Qaeda* fighters were captured or killed but *bin Laden* managed to escape. He remained at large until 2nd May 2011 when he was finally tracked down by United States Intelligence forces to a private compound in Abbottabad, Pakistan. He was shot and killed. His body was buried in the Arabian Sea in order to avoid his resting place becoming a place of pilgrimage.

Conclusion

In Chapter Four we looked at how Islamism replaced Arab Nationalism as a uniting force for many Muslims in the modern world. In this chapter we have seen how Islamism has since developed elements of radical extremism, an example being the rise of *Al-Qaeda* in the 1990s. While *Al Qaeda* was by no means the only extremist group to emerge over the past fifty years, it is the one that has been given the highest profile alongside *Osama bin Laden,* its founder.

Unlike earlier influential Islamic thinkers such as *Ibn Taymiyya,* who was frequently quoted by *Osama,* or *Al Afghani, bin Laden* was not an Islamic scholar. Indeed he has been described as a rather mediocre student who often struggled with his studies at university. What he did have, however, was enormous wealth, a strong charisma and a sense of invincibility, all of which he used to the full.

Bin Laden initially made a name for himself when the Saudi monarchy asked him to raise funds to support Afghanistan against the Soviets. Throughout the ten years' Soviet-Afghan war he could do no wrong in the eyes of the Saudi Government who, along with the United States poured weapons via Pakistan into the hands of *bin Laden* and his Afghan Arab fighters.

When the Soviets withdrew from Afghanistan in 1989 hundreds, if not thousands of Arab Afghan volunteers returned to their home countries where they caused concern for some governments on account of their radical Islamism. *Bin Laden* returned to Saudi Arabia where he was initially welcomed as a hero.

However, everything changed in1990. When Iraq invaded Kuwait on 2 August, *bin Laden* offered to defend the 'Sacred Land of the Two Mosques' (Saudi Arabia) with the help of his fighters. The monarchy rejected his offer in favour of help from the United States. This was to be the tipping point, the moment when the United States became his great enemy alongside Saudi Arabia who he viewed as a puppet of America. When he was stripped of his citizenship in 1992 he spent some time in Sudan where he used his wealth to help the Sudanese on construction projects and continue his recruitment for the global *Jihad.*

After his return to Afghanistan in 1996 he continued to use his wealth and influence to recruit *jihadists* from across the Muslim world. It was during this time that *Al Qaeda* formed its *modus operandi,* which was a formula based on recruitment and training rather than a hierarchical structure.

The most important element of the formula was the *Al Qaeda* worldview, a call for a global and if necessary a violent *Jihad* against all oppressors of Muslims, particularly the United States and her allies. He and his close associates indoctrinated the recruits into this extreme militant radicalism.

Most of the recruits only spent a few months or even weeks in the training camps after which time they returned home. He didn't advise the new *jihadists* which terror acts they should carry out. That was for them to decide according to the local situation. What he had given them was the know-how.

Following the US invasion of Afghanistan in 2001, *Al-Qaeda* lost ground. American bombs killed many *jihadists* but an unknown number escaped to Pakistan and other Muslim countries.

Osama bin Laden was finally killed in 2011 but his death has not resulted in the end of *Al-Qaeda*. His ideology is probably more powerful than ever as we shall see in the following chapter where it has been adopted by the latest, and even more radical expression of militant Islam, that of IS or the so-called Islamic State.

CHAPTER SEVEN

Islamic State of Iraq and Syria (ISIS)/The Islamic State (IS)

We have seen in the previous chapters that modern Islamist thinking emerged at the beginning of the 20th century with the founding of the Muslim Brotherhood. This then spread to other Muslim countries in the region including Saudi Arabia where Brotherhood members, such as *Abdullah Yusuf Azzam,* taught at universities around the country including the *Abdul Aziz* University in Jeddah. Through *Azzam's* teaching *Osama bin Laden* and many others were influenced by the Islamist ideology of the Brotherhood.

Al-Qaeda, which was founded by *bin Laden* in 1988, attracted young Muslims who travelled to his training camps in Afghanistan from across the world (Chapter 6). The Islamists subsequently returned to their home countries where they organised themselves in groups of varying sizes that operated independently while being affiliated to *Al-Qaeda* through a common ideology and occasionally an oath of allegiance.

There are now scores of radical militant groups operating across the world, all espousing some form of Islamist ideology. Regardless of the subtle differences between them in terms of their aims and certain points of ideology or theology, they are frequently described as *Wahhabis* (Chapter 3). While these groups certainly espouse elements of *Wahhabi* doctrine, a better description would be *Salafi.*

The *Salafis* take their name from the *Salaf* who are known as the pious ones of the first three generations of Islam. Modern *Salafis* model themselves on the 7th century *Salaf.* They look to the *Qur'an* and certain *Hadith* (Chapter 1) for legitimacy and reject all forms of innovative thinking, rationalism and scholarship of the later centuries of Islamic history. This would be the thinking of ISIS, *Al-Qaeda*, the *Taliban* and almost all other militant Islamist group.

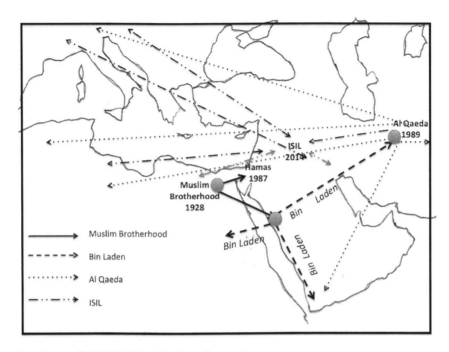

Origins of ISIS/ISIL: *Al-Qaeda* in Iraq

The origins of ISIS can be traced back to the founding in 1999 of a group calling itself *Jama'at al-Tawhid wal-Jihad (*Organisation of Monotheism and *Jihad*). The group was founded by *Abu Musab al-Zarqawi* (1966-2006), a militant Islamist from Jordan. Along with the majority of Islamists, he opposed the presence of US and Western forces on Muslim soil and US support for Israel. He also aimed to topple of the Jordanian monarchy which he considered to be un-Islamic and pro-Western.

For some years *al-Zarqawi* ran a training camp in Afghanistan that was funded by *Osama bin Laden* but when the US invaded Iraq in 2003 he travelled to Iraq in order to fight the occupying forces there. Soon after his arrival in he started to organise travel for hundreds of *Al-Qaeda* operatives who would pass through Syria into Iraq. In this way the country witnessed a growing presence of *Al-Qaeda* militants, a situation that was unknown during the rule of *Saddam Hussein.*

In 2004 *al-Zarqawi* swore allegiance to *Osama bin Laden* so allying himself with *Al-Qaeda*. His group then changed its name to *Tanzim Qaidat al-Jihad fi Bilad al-Rafidayn* also known as '*Al-Qaeda* in Iraq' (AQI) and *al-Zarqawi* was known as 'Emir' of the militant Islamists in Iraq.

Al-Zarqawi and his AQI followers were known for their extreme violence, including suicide bombings, kidnapping and beheadings, all targeted at anyone who did not agree with their ideology. This would include supporters of the Iraqi Government, the US and allied forces and the *Shi'a*. According to reports *al-Zarqawi* personally beheaded American Nick Berg in May 2004 in retaliation for US treatment of prisoners at *Abu Ghraib* prison in the *Al Anbar* Governorate of Iraq.

In 2006 AQI merged with other Sunni militant groups to form the *Mujahideen Shura Council* calling itself the *Islamic State of Iraq* (ISI). At this time *Abu Bakr Al-Baghdadi Al-Qurashi,* better known today as *Al-Baghdadi*, the self-proclaimed Caliph of ISIS, was a committee member of the newly formed ISI. In June of the same year *al-Zarqawi,* founder of AQI, was killed by US forces.

Abu Bakr Al-Baghdadi Al-Qurashi,

Between 2006 and 2010 ISI went into decline, largely as a result of successful US and allied campaigns. However, with the appointment on 10 May 2010 of *Abu Bakr Al-Baghdadi* as leader of ISI, the group began to regain ground.

Al-Baghdadi was born in 1971 in Samarra, an ancient city approximately 78 miles north of Baghdad, which was once the capital of the Abbasid Caliphate. Little is known of his background and consequently various accounts are given of his personal life. This has resulted in him becoming something of a mythic character, which, along with the fact that he is rarely seen in public, adds to his mystique.

According to his contemporaries, as a young man *al-Baghdadi* was shy and retiring. Rather like *Osama bin Laden* he had always been interested in religion and his only other interest was football. There is general agreement that he obtained a Doctorate from the University of Baghdad but uncertainty as to whether this was in education or Islamic studies.

Opinions differ as to *al-Baghdadi's* marital status and whether he has two or three wives. This would not normally be important apart from the fact that the third wife, a woman called *Saja al-Dulaimi,* is currently being held in a Lebanese prison on charges of terrorism. She has also been the subject of a possible hostage exchange.

It is known that between 2004 and 2009 US Forces arrested *al-Baghdadi* as a 'low grade' suspect, but accounts vary as to the exact time he spent in detention. What does seem likely, however, is that this experience led to his radicalisation and changed him from being an unimpressive religious scholar to a violent Islamist.

As leader of ISI (Islamic State in Iraq) *al-Baghdadi* was responsible for numerous attacks on US and Iraqi Government forces as well as attacks on both Sunni and Shi'a mosques. The group also threatened vengeance for the death of *Osama bin Laden* by carrying out bombing raids and suicide attacks.

Islamic State In Syria (ISIS)

When the Syrian Civil War broke out in March 2011 it soon became clear that those who opposed the government of President Assad were unable to form a united front. Initially the Free Syrian Army gained the greatest support from the people and also from the international community. However, the Free Syrian Army fragmented and other opposition groups subsequently were formed including the Islamic Front and the Syrian Revolutionary Command Council, which is a body comprising more than fifty different factions.

The situation became even more complex when, in August 2011 *al-Baghdadi* began sending members of ISI across the border into Syria. Once in Syria they formed a group known as the *Al Nusra* Front, which then became affiliated to *Al Qaeda*.

In April 2013 *al-Baghdadi* announced that from its foundation *al-Nusra* Front had been financed and supported by ISI (the Islamic State of Iraq). *Al-Baghdadi* further claimed that the two organisations had merged to form the 'Islamic State of Iraq and al-Sham' (ISIS). *Al-Nusra* vehemently denied the merger and *al-Qaeda's* leader *al-Zawahiri* also ruled against it. When *al-Baghdadi* ignored the ruling, *al-Qaeda* broke off all official relations with ISIS/ISIL.

Islamic State (IS)

Following the split with *al-Qaeda*, on 29 June 2014, ISIS proclaimed a worldwide Caliphate calling itself the 'Islamic State' with *al-Baghdadi* named as Caliph. This so-called 'Caliphate' claimed religious and political authority over Muslims worldwide. It is a claim that is rejected by the majority of Muslim governments and Muslim leaders who refuse to call the group the 'Islamic State'. Instead, they use the Arabic term *daesh,* which stands for 'The State of Islam in Iraq and the Sham' and is something of a derogatory term.

The primary aim of the 'Islamic State' is to restore the caliphate of the *Umayyad* Dynasty (661-750 CE), whose territory extended from Iran to Spain (Chapter Two). At the time of writing (February 2015) it is estimated that somewhere between eight and twelve million people are living in territory under IS rule.

The professed 'ideology' of IS claims to mirror the beliefs and practices of the first generations of Muslims, known as the 'pious ones', also referred to as the *Salafis* that were mentioned at the beginning of this chapter.

In the process of restoring the Caliphate IS seeks to destroy all the current national boundaries that were established by the *Sykes-Picot Agreement* of 1916 (Chapter Four). Since *Salafis* also reject any form of monarchy as being un-Islamic it views the monarchies of Jordan and Saudi Arabia as illegitimate.

```
Al-Qaeda in Iraq (AQI)  2004
Abu Musab al-Zarqawi


Islamic State of Iraq (ISI)  2006


Islamic State of Iraq and al-Sham (ISIS)  2013
[or Islamic State of Iraq and Levant (ISIL)] 2013
Abu Bakr Al-Baghdadi Al-Qurashi


Islamic State (IS)  2014
[The State of Islam in Iraq and the Sham Region (DAESH)]
Abu Bakr Al-Baghdadi Al-Qurashi
```

RECRUITMENT TO THE ISLAMIC STATE

Those who make up the ranks of IS fall into four categories: a) **previous militants** of *al-Zarqawi's Jama'at al-Tawhid wal-Jihad* or *al-Baghdadi's al-Qaeda* in Iraq; b) **freed prisoners** previously detained by the US/UK forces; c) **local Iraqis and Syrians** who are either forced to join under threat of violence or are bribed; d) **overseas recruits** and volunteers.

Freed Prisoners

Following the US invasion of Iraq in 2003 and the subsequent fall of Saddam Hussein, the Iraqi army was disbanded and hundreds of Iraqi soldiers and *Ba'ath* (Arab Socialist) Party members, who had previously held key positions in the Iraqi government, were imprisoned. In this way the entire infrastructure of Iraq was destroyed and many innocent people arrested.

Apart from feeling a strong sense of injustice at being imprisoned by foreign forces in their own country, many of these prisoners became radicalised. The subsequent revelations of mistreatment of Iraqi prisoners at *Abu Ghraib* added further to their radicalisation.

In 2010 *al-Baghdadi*'s group *'al-Qaeda* in Iraq' stormed many of the prisons releasing army personnel and *Ba'ath* party members. These are the men who went on to become the hardcore of IS. They are men with military and administrative expertise. Ex-Iraqi army officers who became radicalised during the US/UK 'occupation' are now heading the IS army with the aid of tanks and armory once belonging to the Americans or captured from the current Iraqi or Syrian army.

Ex-government officials of the *Ba'ath* party now hold key positions in the structure of IS. Neither the ex-army officers nor the *Ba'ath* party members are likely to be in the front line of the fighting and they would not all be motivated by the *Salafi* ideology but as *Sunnis* many would prefer supporting *Sunni* IS over what they see as an Iraqi 'failed state' that is dominated by the *Shi'a*.

Local Iraqis and Syrians

The third category of recruits are local Iraqis and Syrians who live in territory that has fallen under the control of IS. In this situation many have been forced to co-operate with the terror group or face certain death. Others, particularly young boys, have been offered money and have subsequently become indoctrinated into the *Salafi* ideology.

Overseas recruits

The fourth group is made up of the overseas recruits. They can be divided into two: the professionals and the volunteers. The professionals are doctors, engineers, IT experts etc. who are sympathetic to the IS cause and respond to IS advertisements. Their expertise is vital to IS and consequently they may be offered good salaries and conditions.

Initially the unpaid volunteers were those who were moved by the plight of the Syrian people caught up in the Civil War. They travelled to Syria either to join the Free Syrian Army in the fight against President Assad or to offer their services as doctors or for other humanitarian causes. This is similar to the situation in 1936 when over a period of some three years 35,000 men and women from over 50 countries travelled to Spain to support the Republican fight against the Fascist rule of General Franco.

The volunteers who went to Syria cause the greatest concern for Western governments. The fear is that having become radicalised they will return to their home countries with the intention of carrying out similar terror acts on home soil. Unfortunately many volunteers, even those who went for humanitarian reasons, found themselves caught up with the militant groups. Consequently they found it difficult, if not impossible, to return to their home countries where they were usually viewed as terror suspects and imprisoned.

Finally there are those volunteers from across the world who have responded to the IS propaganda machine. They come from a variety of backgrounds but they are all motivated by a misguided sense of adventure. Through sophisticated videos and on-line sites, young men and women have been enticed into believing that life will be better under *Sharia* Law in a restored Caliphate where they will all be valued as Muslims. In this way they become indoctrinated into the *Salafi* ideology, which they believe justifies the use of the most extreme violence. Those who have already travelled to Syria or Iraq encourage their friends at home to do the same.

Jihadi Brides

Apart from fighters, technicians and doctors, IS needs women to be loyal *jihadi* wives and mothers in order to provide a new generation of *Salafis* so that the Caliphate can be strengthened and grow. Some Syrian and Iraqi women have been forced into marriage. This includes Christian women who have been made to convert to Islam before marriage.

However, an increasing number of *Jihadi* brides are from Europe. It is unknown exactly how many women have travelled to Syria but according to the King's College International Centre for Radicalisation based in London, it is thought that about 1,000 British men have joined IS and over sixty women from across Europe have either travelled to Syria or attempted to do so. The majority of these women are British.

Much of the recruitment is carried out on-line and research shows that there is no shortage of young girls who are attracted by the thought of marriage to a *jihadi* fighter, the prospect of children and life in the Caliphate. Investigations also show that the majority of these girls view such a life as an escape from boredom or an over-controlling family and limited freedom. A few European girls have returned home but for the majority this is not an option.

Research also shows that British women, who are aged between 18 and 24, are at the forefront of the recruitment campaign and also play a key role in the IS Sharia Police Force. In this capacity they are responsible for forcing women to conform to strict Islamic dress, searching burka-clad women for signs of espionage and monitoring any form of 'Western' behaviour.

It has also been reported by the think tank Middle East Media Research Institute (MEMRI), that some British women supervise brothels that house Yazidi women and girls who have been kidnapped by IS fighters and used as sex slaves. IS believes that since these women are not Muslim they can be abused in this way.

Conclusion

In terms of modern Islamist ideology it is possible to trace a direct line of influence from Egypt's Muslim Brotherhood to *Al-Qaeda* in Afghanistan via *Osama bin Laden.* With *bin Laden's* money and influence he was able to recruit *jihadists* from across the world who travelled to training camps in Afghanistan. Although *Al-Qaeda*, as a 'base' has been weakened in recent years, its *Salafi* ideology has continued to spread through a network of an unknown number of militant groups across all parts of the world.

These groups can vary from just two or three individuals to several hundreds or even thousands in the case of IS. However, what has changed in recent years is the mode of indoctrination. Instead of travelling to training camps, today aspiring *jihadists* can simply log on to the World Wide Web.

Many Muslims around the world were angered by the US and allied invasion of Iraq in 2003. The subsequent occupation of Iraq by foreign forces and the humiliation suffered by the Iraqi people was considered to be justification by militant Islamists for *jihad*. As a result, hundreds of *jihadis* joined *Al-Zakawi* and his group *Al-Qaeda* in Iraq (AQI).

The dismantling of the Iraqi army and government infrastructure by the occupying forces resulted in a power vacuum that was quickly filled by competing groups, including *Al-Qaeda* elements. At the same time some of the key military and government personnel were imprisoned, an experience that led to their radicalisation, as was the case with *Al-Baghdadhi*. AQI stormed the prisons and liberated hundreds of inmates, some of whom later assumed key roles in IS.

When the Syrian Civil War erupted in 2011 the main opposition group, the Free Syrian Army, was unable to maintain a united front. *Al-Qaeda* in Iraq once more took advantage of the resulting power vacuum. AQI moved across the border into Syria. Here it confronted the government forces of President Assad and also came into conflict with the various opposition groups as each group contended for power.

We have commented on how the modern *Salafi* ideology has spread and also how the different militant groups were formed in the context of the invasion of Iraq and the Syrian civil war.

The question that now needs to be asked is why so many Muslims have felt compelled to join militant groups such as IS, a group that is condemned by Islamic governments and leaders from around the world because of its betrayal of Islam and its extreme brutality

It might be easier to understand why Iraqis and Syrians living in the region have fallen prey to extremist groups. The Iraqis in particular suffered during the foreign occupation resulting in many developing a hatred for the West. Others became radicalised while in US/UK detention. Sectarianism also played a part. For example, some *Sunni* tribes decided to support IS rather than the *Shi'a* dominated Iraqi government by whom they felt maginalised.

The situation in Syria is somewhat different. At the outbreak of the civil war many moderate Muslims joined the opposition to President Assad. But when *Al- Baghdadi* began sending his *Al Qaeda* militants over the border into Syria some moderate Syrians were forced through various means to join the *jihadis*.

The big question that faces many western governments is 'why should so many young Muslims who were born and educated in Europe, Australia or other parts of the world choose to travel to a dangerous war zone where they could very well be killed?   Although coming from different cultures and countries and allowing for the fact that they will have their own personal reasons, the one thing that seems common to all is a sense of alienation within their own community.

Ever since the bombing of the Twin Towers on 11 September 2001 an increasing number of young male Muslims have felt that they are perceived as suspect terrorists. Unfortunately as politicians ratchet up the war against terror and the rhetoric increases, this alienation leads to further possible radicalisation, thereby creating a vicious cycle.

CONCLUSION

In the prologue to this book I explained that the impetus for writing it was my horror at the brutal beheading of American journalist James Foley on 19 August 2014. Since that time there have been a further 14 known beheadings of individuals by ISIS. As well as these individual executions, an unknown number of Syrians, Iraqis and Afghans have also been murdered in a similar way. The latest atrocity occurred on 15 February 2015 when ISIS beheaded 21 Egyptian Coptic Christians on a Libyan beach. At the same time sporadic terror attacks have increased in European and other Western cities.

Apart from beheadings, hundreds, if not thousands of women and girls have been sold into slavery, used as sex slaves, have been raped or forced into marriages. According to *Al-Monitor,* during the twelve months following the Geneva II Conference held in January 2014, a further 100,000 people have died in Syria and the number of foreign fighters in Syria has jumped from 7,500 to over 20,000.

My reason for writing this book has been to try and 'make sense' of this form of militant extremism that claims legitimacy for such brutality in the name of Islam. While not anticipating finding satisfactory answers to my questions, I hoped, by the end, to better understand the phenomenon of radical and militant Islamism. I particularly wanted to explore what motivated the *jihadists*, to discover their aims and understand how they could justify their brutal acts.

From the perspective of the *jihadist*, the answer to all three questions relating to motivation, aims and justification would lie in his or her particular understanding of Islam. In other words, ideology forms the basis upon which all else is founded. I therefore began the book by comparing a mainstream 'traditional' view of Islam with the ideological worldview of modern militant Islamists.

The Ideology

The Qur'an, the *Hadith* and the *Sunnah* are the basis for Muslim belief and practice as well as the foundation of Islamic religious law. Interpretation of the sacred texts has traditionally been the responsibility of religious scholars and judges. As the Faith spread beyond the Arabian Peninsula during the late 6th and early 7th centuries, different schools of interpretation known as *madhhabs* evolved, reflecting different social and historical contexts.

These schools, which were founded by eminent religious scholars, played a vital part in ensuring the legitimacy of the *hadith* and an interpretation of the text for a given situation. Still today, Islamic scholars in prestigious universities such as *Al-Azhar* in Cairo continue their work on the early *hadith.*

Over the centuries a large amount of scholarship has been accumulated, much of which involves pronouncements on what is, or what is not, permissible in Islamic law. In their effort to relate Islam to the modern world scholars will come to a consensus of opinion and make a pronouncement (*fatwa*) without compromising the original Qur'anic text. Sometimes scholars will conclude that a particular *hadith* is no longer relevant or has been superseded.

Modern radical Islamists however reject the scholarship of the *madhhabs* on the grounds that it is pure human innovation. For them all that is necessary is the Qur'an and a limited, very early selection of *hadith.* They will take a selective and literalist view of a Qur'anic text regardless of historical context. Consequently they are able to justify carrying out barbaric practices that were the norm in 6th century Arabia.

Many militant Islamists refer to the works of *Ibn Taymiyya* in order to legitimise their actions. However this is to misunderstand both the man and his writings. As we saw in Chapter 3, *Ibn Taymiyya* (1268-1328) was a highly educated philosopher, scholar and logician. He developed his theory of militant *jihad* in the context of a particular threat from the Mongols that was not necessarily binding for all time. Above all, he opposed the killing of defenceless people and especially women and children.

Unlike the majority of Muslims who would follow the tradition of a particular *madhhab*, militant Islamists are encouraged to practice 'independent reasoning' (*ijtihad*). While 'independent reasoning' might be appropriate for a scholarly mind such as *Ibn Taymiyya* it can be extremely dangerous when practiced by the uneducated. Despite this, the Muslim Brotherhood and *Osama bin Laden* encouraged *ijtihad*, as do their heirs ISIS, and other similar groups such as *Boco Haram* and *al-Shabaab.*

When the theory of *ijtihad* is put into practice by the unqualified and uneducated, the results can be disastrous as we are seeing today in ISIS controlled territory. Furthermore when individuals remove themselves from their social environment, as is the case with *jihadis* travelling to Syria from many parts of the world, all normal social controls such as family and community are removed. This may leave them feeling uninhibited and free from the social norms that, together with a false sense of liberation, allows them to commit such hideous acts as beheading.

The majority of the world's Muslims view the rise of this form of radical Islam, which permits the mass murder of innocent people, with horror. They claim that since the militants' actions are based upon an incorrect interpretation of the Qur'an and *hadith* then it is un-Islamic and the militants are not 'true' Muslims.

In response to the rise of militant Islam, many Muslim leaders have issued *fatwas* denouncing ISIS. Unfortunately these are usually issued in Arabic and therefore not accessible to the hundreds of non-Arabic speaking *jihadists* and potential *jihadists* from around the world who are attracted by ISIS ideology. In an attempt to address this situation a joint initiative has been taken by the British Council and *Al-Azhar* University in Cairo. This involves extensive training, funded by the British Council, of young Muslim scholars in the English language. It is hoped that the University will then be able to publish counter-arguments to extreme *Salafi* teaching that will be accessible to Muslims worldwide.

The Historical Background

Generally speaking Muslims have a very strong sense of history. They remember the early centuries of expansion under the *Umayyads* (661-750CE) and the scientific and cultural achievements of the *Abbasids* (750-1258CE). Then came the Ottomans, who conquered large parts of Eastern Europe and had a navy that gave them supremacy over the Eastern Mediterranean Sea.

By the beginning of the 19th century the Muslim world was in decline. The dissolution of the Ottoman Empire in 1923 marked the end of the Caliphate. Although by that time many regions of the Empire had achieved autonomous rule, nevertheless Istanbul remained a potent symbol of Islamic unity. With the dissolution of the Empire that focal point was lost. A power vacuum emerged into which various factions have competed for power, the latest being ISIS.

Many Muslims have asked themselves why and how the Muslim world has so declined. The *Salafis*, those who look back to the first generations of Islam as a 'golden age', believe that it was because of the corrupt and despotic rule of its leaders who were promoting 'Western' ways. Consequently, *Salafis* believe that these rulers, many of whom they view as 'puppets' of the West, should be overthrown.

They also believe that Islam needs 'reforming' in order to restore the purity of the first generations. The majority of today's militant Islamists follow this *Salafi* thinking and consequently their aim is to overthrow current Islamic monarchies and governments and restore the early *Umayyad* Caliphate. In their eyes those who oppose these aims are considered an enemy against whom it is a duty to wage *jihad*. The 'enemy' would include all non-Muslims and also those Muslims who do not subscribe to their particular form of Islam.

A more common response to the decline of the Islamic world, held by many Muslims, is to blame Western imperialism. Both the Ottoman and the Mughal Empires suffered a loss in trade as a result of European colonisation during the 19th century. The real catastrophe, however, was the *Sykes-Picot* Agreement of 6th May 1916 when France, Britain and Russia carved up parts of the Ottoman Empire into 'spheres of influence'. In the process artificial borders were drawn across territories regardless of cultural history and tribal affiliation.

The other 'running sore' for Muslims worldwide is the on-going suffering of their fellow Muslim Palestinians who they believe have been deprived of their homeland and have lived under Israeli occupation since 1948.

Post 9/11

On 20 September 2001 US President George W Bush declared a 'War on Terror'. This was in response to the bombing of the Twin Towers a few days earlier, on the 11th September. The UK and other Western countries immediately joined in the war cry.

Despite the fact that world leaders repeatedly stressed that this was a war against terror and not against Islam, this differentiation has not been heard by many in the Muslim world. Consequently some non-Muslims have been unable to differentiate between a Muslim and a terrorist. This was played out in the days following 9/11 when there were numerous accounts of innocent Muslims, both male and female, being attacked in the streets of UK and US towns and cities.

The US invasion of Afghanistan in response to 9/11 and the search for *Osama bin Laden,* once more led to the suffering of innocent Muslims. Apart from allied forces, some 15,000 Afghan National Security Forces were killed. No one knows how many innocent Afghan civilians, including women and children, have lost their homes, livelihood and lives since the invasion.

The invasion of Iraq in 2003 and the killing of Saddam Hussein not only led to the deaths, once more, of innocent Iraqis but it also resulted in the dismantling of the military and civil infrastructure of the country. Crucially however, the resulting chaos provided a perfect training ground for future *jihadists*, many of whom moved from Afghanistan to Iraq.

These modern wars are captured in real-time on TV. Noam Chomsky in his book *Failed States* describes how a suspect bomber, when questioned, claimed that his "bomb plot was directly inspired by Britain's involvement in the Iraq war" and how he had "watched hours of TV footage showing grief-stricken Iraqi widows and children alongside images of civilians killed in the conflict." He said that he had a feeling of hatred and a conviction that he had "to do something".

Various intelligence bodies have concluded that the vast majority of foreign fighters in Iraq were not former terrorists but had become radicalised by the war itself to such an extent that they felt compelled to come to the aid of their fellow Muslims in the fight against the 'crusaders' and 'infidels'. Indeed, according to Chomsky, reaction to the invasion of Iraq was so strong in the Muslim world that *Al Azhar* University in Cairo actually issued a *fatwa* advising "all Muslims in the world to make *jihad* against invading American forces".

Since the beginning of the Syrian Civil War in March 2011, hundreds of thousands of innocent Syrians, the majority being Muslims but also including Christians and Kurds, are trapped in a war between four competing forces: President Assad's government forces, a coalition of opposition forces, *Al-Qaeda* affiliated groups such as *Al Nusra Front* and ISIS. As well as these competing ground forces the US and its allies, including Arab nations, are bombing ISIS targets in Syria, which only adds to the misery of the people.

It is into this maelstrom that thousands of *jihadists* from around the world are drawn. Initially many joined the Syrian opposition forces against what they perceived to be the demonic rule of President Assad. But as these opposition forces began to fragment many were drawn into *Al Nusra*. By April 2013 ISIS members had moved across the border from Iraq bringing with them all the military and technical know-how that they had accumulated following the downfall of Saddam Hussein.

ISIS is completely different to *Al Qaeda*. Although both subscribe to the same *Salafi* teaching the two have different aims and therefore different methods. While *Osama bin Laden* promoted the downfall of governments, including both Western governments and the Saudi regime, he had no territorial ambitions. From his base he encouraged potential *jihadists* to travel to his various training camps, whether in Afghanistan, Pakistan, Yemen or East Africa. Here they were indoctrinated into the Al Qaeda worldview, trained in the art of terrorism and then sent home to operate as free agents.

ISIS has different aims and methods. First and foremost it has territorial ambitions in that it aims to establish a Caliphate covering territory similar to that of the early *Umayyads*. In order to do this it needs first of all to recruit an army, many being local fighters but an increasing number are foreign recruits. As part of its recruitment campaign ISIS promotes the concept of a multi-national Islamic army where recruits from all over the world will be welcome. However, on arrival these fresh recruits are quickly indoctrinated into the ISIS ideology and deviation is not tolerated. Neither is it easy to leave.

As well as fighters ISIS depends upon an army of engineers, medics, technicians, indeed all skills that are necessary to run a 'state'. But most of all ISIS needs to ensure that it has a new generation of *jihadis*. Consequently, they kidnap and force girls into marriage and have developed a sophisticated on-line network aimed at luring young girls from Europe to become *jihadi* brides.

The Future?

It has been suggested that the outrageous atrocities committed by militant Islamists, starting with 9/11 and continuing today under ISIS, are aimed at both instilling fear and provoking a reaction. There is no doubt that on both accounts the terrorists have been successful. If not more dangerous today, the world is certainly more fearful, to the extent that a whole new multi-dollar industry has been built up under the umbrella of 'security' services.

When *Al-Qaeda* bombed the Twin Towers, *Osama bin Laden* certainly expected and hoped for a reaction. As he predicted,

President Bush declared a 'War on Terror' that was quickly followed up with US military action. Both *Al-Qaeda* and ISIS are provoking the West into a confrontation. If Western bombs are seen dropping on Muslim towns and cities, causing evermore suffering for innocent civilians, Muslims around the world will become increasingly outraged and some will be inspired to join the *jihad* against the 'crusaders'. What the *jihadists* want most of all is a 'cosmic' war between the West and Islam.

While battles continue to rage in the Middle East a growing number of 'home grown' *jihadists* are committing terror attacks in Western cities. The majority have been radicalised via the Internet and it is increasingly difficult to identify those in danger of radicalisation. There would appear to be no one profile for a potential *jihadist*. They come from a variety of social and educational backgrounds and they do not necessarily show signs of changed behaviour or withdrawal as might be expected of one contemplating joining ISIS or any other terror group. The 'normality' of some young people has been proven in the case of the three young girls who disappeared from an East London school in February 2015, thought to be planning to join ISIS.

While the anti-terror rhetoric continues to rise and increasing anti-terror legislation is put in place, more and more Muslims living in Western countries feel a growing sense of alienation. This sense of alienation is one of the root causes leading to radicalisation.

The war against militant Islam is being waged on several fronts that nevertheless can broadly be divided into two: a military engagement in the Middle East, and an anti-terror intelligence exercise in Western countries. In both arenas any hope of success can only be achieved if not only the 'West' and Muslims can work together, but if the Muslims themselves can overcome their differences and work together.

Many Muslim governments and leaders have openly condemned ISIS. It might be hoped therefore that more Arab countries in the region could join forces against their common enemy. But this is perhaps too simple an answer. Apart from the fact that ISIS sympathisers can be found in all Muslim countries, there remains the age-old *Sunni-Shi'a* tension. A resolution in the foreseeable future therefore seems at once essential, yet equally unobtainable.

GLOSSARY

Ahl al-bayt: Household of the Prophet

Ahl al-Hadith: Sect that takes uncritical view of *Hadith*

AQI: *Al-Qaeda* in Iraq

al-Shabaab: 'Party of Youth' Militant *Salafi* group based in Somalia

Ansar: Helper during the Prophet's period in Medina

Boco Haram: 'Western Education Forbidden' militant terror group based
in Nigeria

Caliph: Successor to the Prophet

DAESH: Arabic term for The State of Islam in Iraq and the Sham Region

Deobandi: *Sunni* revivalist movement found in India and Pakistan

Fatwa: Legal opinion/pronouncement

Hadith: Saying or action attributed to *Muhammad*

Hijra: Emigration of *Muhammad* to Medina 622AD/1AH marking the beginning of the Islamic calendar

ISI: Islamic State in Iraq

ISIL: Islamic State of Iraq and the Levant

ISIS: Islamic State of Iraq and Syria(*al Shams*)

Ijtihad: Independent reasoning

Jihad: Struggle, either spiritual or military

Kaaba: Most sacred mosque and pilgrimage site located at Mecca

Madhhab: 'school' of Islamic jurisprudence

Madrassa: Religious school/college

Mahdi: Future leader prophesied to bring peace and justice

Mufti: Scholar who gives legal pronouncements/*fatwas*

Mujahideen: Group engaged in *jihad*

Mu'tazilis: Philosophical school stressing reason and rational thought

Muwahhidin: A Muslim who believes in the Oneness of God. Also describes some Druze and Berbers

Qadi: Judge

Qutbists: Followers of *Sayyid Qutb* of the Muslim Brotherhood
shari'a Islamic religious Law

Shirk: That which is forbidden, e.g. idolatry or polytheism

Shura: Council

Sufi: A practitioner of the mystical dimension of Islam

Sunnah: Way of life following the practice and teaching of Muhammad

Sunni: Largest branch of Islam/those who follow the tradition of Muhammad and consensus of the *Ummah*

Sura: Chapter of the *Qur'an*

Ulema: Religious scholars

Ummah: The worldwide community of Muslims

WORKS REFERRED TO

Ahmed Rashid, *Taliban,* 2000, I. B. Taurus,

Albert Hourani, *A History of the Arab Peoples*

Al-Monitor: the Pulse of the Middle East on-line journal

E-International Relations website for students of international politics

Jason Burke, *Al-Qaeda,* 2003, Penguin

Jonathan Randal, *Osama,* 2005 I.B. Taurus,

Noam Chomsky, *Failed States,* 2006, Penguin

Salafism: Oxford Bibliographies on-line Research *Guide*

ABOUT THE AUTHOR

Anne has had a life-long interest in history and the religions of the world. This led to her studying both topics for her first Degree and later for her Doctorate. She spent several years living overseas and this experience added to her fascination with people of different Faiths and cultures.

For many years Anne was Adviser in Inter Religious Relations with the Church of England. She was also Vice Moderator of the Dialogue Unit of the World Council of Churches in Geneva and has sat on numerous advisory bodies for Inter Religious Relations around the world. In recognition of her work in this field she was made an Honorary Canon of Chelmsford Cathedral.

Anne lectures regularly on cruise ships and many organisations around the United Kingdom. She is also an Accredited Lecturer with the National Association of Fine Arts Societies.

She now enjoys writing short, accessible books, many of which have been based on her lectures. This book is the culmination of her many years working to improve a better understanding between people of different Faiths. It is the fifth in the *'In Brief'* *Series: Books for Busy People.*

http://www.annedavison.org.uk

10376254R00059

Printed in Great Britain
by Amazon.co.uk, Ltd.,
Marston Gate.